Psychosocial Interventions *for* GENETICALLY INFLUENCED PROBLEMS *in* Childhood *and* Adolescence

Psychosocial Interventions *for* GENETICALLY INFLUENCED PROBLEMS *in* Childhood *and* Adolescence

Richard Rende

WILEY

Cover image: © romainainjl/iStockphoto
Cover design: Wiley

This book is printed on acid-free paper. ♾

Published by John Wiley & Sons, Inc., Hoboken, New Jersey.
Published simultaneously in Canada.

For general information on our other products and services please contact our Customer Care Department within the United States at (800) 762-2974, outside the United States at (317) 572-3993 or fax (317) 572-4002.

Wiley publishes in a variety of print and electronic formats and by print-on-demand. Some material included with standard print versions of this book may not be included in e-books or in print-on-demand. If this book refers to media such as a CD or DVD that is not included in the version you purchased, you may download this material at http://booksupport.wiley.com. For more information about Wiley products, visit www.wiley.com.

Library of Congress Cataloging-in-Publication Data:

Rende, Richard.
Psychosocial interventions for genetically influenced problems in childhood and adolescence / Richard Rende.
pages cm
Includes bibliographical references and index.
ISBN 978-1-118-01699-2 (paperback); ISBN 9781-118-23569-0 (ebk); ISBN 978-1-118-22199-0 (ebk)
1. Child psychopathology–Genetic aspects. 2. Adolescent psychopathology–Genetic aspects. I. Title.
RJ499.R43 2015
618.92'89042–dc23

2014013657

Printed in the United States of America

10 9 8 7 6 5 4 3 2 1

Contents

Preface

We assume genes play a role in all behavioral and emotional disorders of childhood and adolescence. The magnitude of the genetic impact, the processes underlying how genes contribute to both risk and protection, and the ways in which genes and environments intersect have all been investigated intensively over the past two decades. What are the implications of this ongoing work for preventing and treating children and adolescents now and in the future?

When the Human Genome Project (HGP) was completed – over a decade ago – there were claims (and perhaps promises) that identification of genes would revolutionize treatment. We envisioned that gene discovery would lead to the development of biological techniques that target those genes (or the effects of those genes) in a fundamental way. Gene discovery would also rewrite how we diagnose disorders – including the behavioral and emotional disorders of childhood and adolescence – leading to more valid identification of risk processes that could be eradicated biologically. A similar idea – but perhaps one with more tempered expectations – is that gene identification would at least lead to a clearer identification of individuals at risk for disorder and provide a platform for treatments tailored to their DNA profile.

While these various perspectives were in a sense the promised deliverables of HGP, we have not yet seen the realization of that promise. We are finding that the etiology is more elusive than anticipated by HGP, and more in line with prior conceptual models of complex disorders. *Many* genes are typically involved, none of which is so independently and directly responsible to warrant our thinking that it can be "manipulated" biologically to fully or substantially reduce risk. These multiple genes all operate in the context of robust environmental influences. There is emerging evidence of how genes and environment intersect. It may be argued that one important deliverable of the HGP, relative to behavioral and emotional disorders, is to confirm what we had thought previously – that the etiology of every disorder is multifactorial with influences arising at both the genetic and environmental level.

Since we know that both genes and environment are at play, what are the implications for prevention and intervention? To begin, we need to eliminate the word "promise" from our discussions of genetics as applied to prevention and intervention. Genetically tailored biological interventions are simply a possibility, perhaps an unlikely one given the number of etiological influences that underlie behavioral and emotional disorders. Another possibility – one that is argued here to be more realistic – is that psychosocial interventions hold the most promise for making substantial traction in prevention and intervention efforts.

That is not to say that genetic research will not be influential. Our accumulating understanding of genetics will in fact help us devise and implement more effective psychosocial interventions. The last decade has witnessed unprecedented growth in empirical efforts to understand the joint effects of genes and environment. While this work has also proven to yield somewhat murky results at times, overall the overwhelming conclusion is that we need more, not less, approaches that cast gene effects in relevant psychosocial contexts. Even more compelling is the idea that, when we step back and have a good look at the evidence to date and the emerging conceptual models that both support this line of research and continue to evolve from it, gene–environment studies indicate that the best way to alter the developmental trajectories of youth at high genetic risk for behavioral and emotional disorders is to change their environment. And a critically important way to support that goal is to continue to study genetics – but only if the deliverables of the DNA laboratories are not divorced from the need to deliver and improve psychosocial interventions that hold promise for immediate and long-term improvement in the functioning of children and adolescents.

Here we take a highly selective look at research on genes and environments to ascertain different models of how genetic research may inform psychosocial interventions – and why psychosocial interventions are taking on greater importance post HGP. We consider autism spectrum disorder (ASD), attention-deficit/hyperactivity disorder (ADHD) and reading disorder (RD), conduct problems (CP) and substance use (SU), depression (MDD), pediatric bipolar disorders (PBD), and anxiety disorders (AD). In each chapter, one major theme from ongoing research is highlighted to illuminate a principle about how the environment matters, why we should learn more about it, and why it might provide the most likely route for prevention and intervention. For example, research on ASD will highlight the complexities of gene identification for this disorder – and the compelling new evidence that gene–brain-behavior pathways may be altered by carefully crafted and intensive psychosocial interventions. While we think of ADHD and RD as highly heritable disorders, current thinking suggests that this doesn't mean that their expression is not substantially influenced by environmental context – and that the psychosocial environment offers much room for modifying the effects of these disorders on development. Both conduct problems and substance use have been shown to reflect environmental factors that lead to similar behaviors in family members (shared environment) – and current promising psychosocial interventions are shown to target hypothesized shared environmental processes. Depression runs in families – and treatments that reduce levels of depression in parents offer similar direct benefits on their children via changes in parenting. Pediatric bipolar disorder is a complex disorder that typically arises in a very complex context of environmental risk – yet we haven't seen enough support for developing psychosocial interventions especially given that there are few biological treatments that are optimally effective. And a consideration of the anxiety disorders reveals intriguing evidence that environmental traumas not only act on genetic vulnerabilities but may in fact alter gene expression through the lifespan – leading to a consideration that early interventions may help undermine this maladaptive biological process.

The real promise for the future will lie in accelerated efforts to apply, refine, and develop psychosocial interventions using our interdisciplinary knowledge base on genes, environments, and their interplay across developmental time. It's time to abandon another round of promises about the deliverables of genetic research that aren't expected to pay off for decades. In contrast, psychosocial interventions have been shown to be effective in the here and now – and by more fully investing in their potential we can learn even more about genetics while evolving more effective interventions that hold promise for improving children's lives today.

Acknowledgments

Writing a book that offers speculations about the future of genetics and intervention is a dicey proposition. Both fields provide moving targets as new (and potentially unexpected) findings can dramatically alter our perspective. Thus, I am particularly grateful to Patricia Rossi for her extraordinary guidance – and patience – as an editor who navigated the interesting process of deciding when it felt right to say that we were done.

Psychosocial Interventions *for* GENETICALLY INFLUENCED PROBLEMS *in* Childhood *and* Adolescence

CHAPTER

1

Prelude: Great Expectations

Over a decade ago, when the race to decode the human genome was in full stride, the expectations were great – and then some. The rhetoric focused not on the possibility, but on the promise, that the Human Genome Project (HGP) would revolutionize clinical practice, including the diagnosis and treatment of developmental, behavioral, and emotional disorders in infancy, childhood, and adolescence. This was no basic science endeavor focused on an intellectual holy grail. The HGP came with a very large promissory note – to uncover the genetic origins of disease and disorder and point directly and quickly to biological interventions that would have unprecedented success.

Once the completion of the HGP was formally announced in 2003, the expectations were that we would now be positioned to find the answers to questions that genetic research had promised (and failed) to answer in the past. The primary questions that lingered centered on the speed and scope of the impact. Would the knowledge derived from the HGP lead to "magic bullet" therapies that could inhibit pathological processes caused by rogue genes? Or would it lead to a better understanding of the role that genes play in disease and rapidly inform us about strategies that could be taken to compensate for genetic risk? In either case, we would have the knowledge to either circumvent or inhibit deleterious genetic influences by biological means, or at a minimum develop tailored interventions that would scan your DNA and tell you how to prevent, or eradicate, a pathological condition. The question that was harder to envision back then – now a decade ago – was whether it would simply illustrate how difficult it would be to move from identifying pathogenic genes to actually doing something about them or, for that matter, even actually identifying those genes.

These questions were prominent in the minds of those who study developmental, behavioral, and emotional disorders in children and adolescents. During the 1990s, there had been an explosion of research that used genetic methods and concepts in developmental psychopathology. Behavioral genetic approaches (such as twin and adoption studies) generated an impressive amount of informative data that were consistent with the idea that DNA is implicated in virtually every form of child and adolescent psychopathology. So just like researchers and practitioners who studied cancer or heart disease, developmental psychopathologists eagerly awaited to see how the HGP would transform what we do, and most importantly, how it would impact our ability to improve children's lives. And this wasn't just speculation. Go back a decade, and you will see that nearly every major longitudinal study of childhood psychopathology made some level of investment in the collection of DNA, in anticipation of some type of major advancement.

So, where do we stand right now? A quick Internet search today will reveal that the HGP revolution – with respect to intervention – has not happened. Numerous articles in the popular press over the past few years have documented the very gradual slope involved in identifying disease genes that could inform new therapeutic techniques. Some have drawn an analogy to business bubbles, in that the great expectations that surrounded the HGP has given way to the sober reality that a decade later few (if any) radical advances have been made with respect to therapeutics. *National Geographic* ran a piece that focused on the five breakthroughs from the HGP and five predictions. Developing gene therapies to cure disease was listed as a *prediction* – not a breakthrough – as it was proposed that this could *start happening* sometime in the *next* decade (or two decades after the completion of the HGP).

One could speculate that the popular press may be inclined to skew perceptions. However, the collective voice extends to the world of science. In July 2011, the prestigious journal *Human Genetics* devoted a special section to the yield to date of the HGP with respect to intervention. It included articles such as "*Translating Human Genomics into Population Screening: Hype or Hope?*" Other papers focused on the substantial challenges that scientists anticipate in moving from the extraordinary knowledge base derived from the HGP to the ultimate deliverable: genetically informed and tailored treatment strategies that work for a range of diseases. Even Francis Collins, who led the HGP initiative at the National Institutes of Health, has acknowledged in multiple interviews that the HGP has not had the massive immediate practical impact on treatment and prevention that was anticipated by many during the years that culminated in the announcement that the human genome was decoded.

But now there's even more to consider as the DNA story gets more tangled and complex. More than 30 papers were published in concert in September 2012 to disseminate the newest thinking about the genome and how genes influence development in the broadest sense. This research initiative called ENCODE is focused on extensive regions in DNA that were thought to be, well, junk – and reflects a new "encyclopedia" of DNA that radically alters that viewpoint. You may have heard that only 20% of DNA is actually doing something. Well, the new research is showing that nearly 80% of DNA is doing something (or more technically, has been assigned a biochemical function). The spotlight is not just on the genes that code for proteins, but also the vast number of genes that act as switches that turn other genes on and off. This regulatory function has been known for a long time, and its importance has always been grasped. What's different now is that it seems to be a predominant mechanism with many genes – and big chunks of DNA – devoted to it. And researchers believe that the emerging ENCODE may hold clues to understanding how many disorders arise from expression of genetic risk factors along with a whole potential range of factors. What is really changing is the emerging idea that it's not so much what is in the "core" genes that directly code for things, but rather how the complex mix of influences that turn genes on and off takes place continuously throughout development.

If you peruse the commentary of scientists involved with ENCODE, it's clear that the genetic landscape is getting more and more complicated, with more and more interplay between lots of genes and gene regions, and more and more unspecified influences that impact how genes have their influence on development and pathology. One analogy has been made to the genome being a "jungle" full of layers of biological factors that, at any given time, may be interacting in almost incalculable ways. You can think about it as multiple orchestras with lots of instruments and plenty of conductors. But whatever analogy you like, the big point is that while this new thinking on DNA – reflecting the work of something like 400 scientists over the last 8 years – is certainly extraordinary, it raises even more questions about how quickly we are going to translate knowledge about genetics into biologically informed prevention and intervention. In that sense, the idea that identifying a "disease" gene for complicated disorders, as informed by the HGP, will lead to a direct implication for diagnosis and treatment starts to sound less and less feasible in the near future (at a minimum).

Let's step back for a minute. Should you be thinking that this is a rant about genetics, or the slow pace of science, or the fact that it seems like every decade we come across a new "breakthrough" in thinking and methods that doesn't actually lead to anything practical for the vast majority of affected individuals? Not at all. That's how science typically works, and genetic research is no exception. This is about our great expectations of what genetic knowledge will do for us, which frankly may have been oversold in the scientific community. We had heard it before, but just the idea of the HGP – the thought that we would know all the genes – raised the stakes and expectations accordingly. Let's face it – we've invested not just extraordinary monetary and scientific resources in the HGP, but also faith and hope that led to expectations for immediate results. And while breakthroughs may happen, the stark reality is that they might not happen any time soon.

This reality is especially sobering when we consider the developmental, behavioral, and emotional disorders of childhood and adolescence. Why? Simply put, parents and practitioners alike deal with the need to change children's lives *today*. Parents don't have a decade to wait for unspecified advances that might happen. Think about how many kids have received a psychiatric diagnosis since the completion of the HGP. When I first learned about autism, the prevalence was estimated to be 4 in 10,000 – now that estimate is something like 1 in 110 (or maybe even 1 in 88). ADHD diagnoses are on the rise, and close to 1 in 10 kids will receive a diagnosis (or maybe even 1 in 7). These diagnoses happen in the first decade of life; so as each decade passes, we have extraordinary numbers of kids who were born who would profit from the development of new interventions. Yet despite all the resources devoted to understanding the genetic basis of some of the most prevalent and impairing disorders that affect youth from birth through adolescence – autism, dyslexia, ADHD, conduct disorder, depression, and substance abuse – the translation of genetic discoveries into new and effective biological interventions has been, at least to my way of thinking, nonexistent.

The overall point is not that genetics research is misguided – far from that. Rather, the viewpoint expressed here is that we have learned from the HGP that the simple equation

Identifying Genes = Biological Intervention

has not been validated over the past decade. We are just starting to learn from the ENCODE project that the genome may involve a complex net of influences that may or may not be easily analyzed. Yet it's not at all clear that the scientific infrastructure – including the world of researchers and funders – has revamped the goals or commitment to genetics. In a world of unlimited funding and support, this wouldn't be a bad thing. However, the reality is that it's time to reconsider what we are learning from genetic research and the extent to which we can put it to use in intervention strategies that are feasible right now – especially when we think about developmental psychopathology.

The premise here is not that the HGP, or ENCODE, or genetic research in general, is a dead end. Far from it. Rather, those of us who deal with trying to improve the emotional, behavioral, and cognitive development of children – some of whom are undoubtedly influenced substantially by genetic factors – need to revisit our intellectual, financial, and emotional attachment to genetics. We need to seriously modify our expectations about how advances in genetic research can inform intervention. We need to consider with more commitment and vigor how our emerging knowledge about genetics can be integrated into nonbiological approaches to treatment – which directs the spotlight to the less sexy world of environmental intervention. Let's toss this thought into the mix: Our accumulated knowledge deriving from genetically informed research may help us shape more powerful environmental interventions that could meaningfully change children's lives today and tomorrow.

The fact is, there are intriguing research directions that are happening right now – and some that have been going on for years – that directly or indirectly demonstrate how we can do something right now to improve kid's lives based on decades of research on genes and environment. Notice I didn't say anything here about revolutionizing our understanding of developmental psychopathology, or curing disorders. The focus is on improvement in functioning, reduction of risk, and coming up with interventions that might work better than what we've done before. The overarching goal is to illuminate exciting new research directions and some long-standing approaches that point the way toward the more likely yield in the near future – sharpening and transforming psychosocial interventions based on what we learn from genetically informed research.

But in order to do that, we need to shake off the pervasive mindset that keeps clinging to the idea that we will keep mucking along with environmental strategies until the "real" science of genetics solves all our problems and makes diseases go away. Why is this necessary? There is just no debating the fact that DNA dominates the behavioral sciences right now in the lay world. You are much more likely to click on the Internet and read about how there is a "mommy gene" that will tell you if a woman wants to be a mother (based on a study of rats) rather than extraordinary work on a promising new psychosocial intervention for autism spectrum disorder (which comes out of our understanding drawn from decades of genetically informative research).

DNA still dominates the world of science and of funding in particular. I haven't done this exercise, but some of you enterprising types might do a little research on the financial commitment to genetic research at the National Institutes of Health as compared to psychosocial research. Take a look at the portfolios over the last decade at the National Institute of

Mental Health and the National Institute on Drug Abuse (to name a few). I would speculate that the dollars backing genetic research greatly surpass those devoted to psychosocial intervention. Our scientific mindset is much more likely to invest heavily in biological interventions for addiction rather than strategies aimed to prevent use. It's a matter of degree and of perception – genetics is hard science, intervention is soft science. Genetics will lead to breakthroughs; intervention will produce modest gains. I've been in the rooms, sat in the meetings, gone to the conferences, read the journals, and contributed to the dialogue both in writing and in person and I have seen directly how we have lost our sense of balance. We are simply not hearing enough about the innovative work that uses principles drawn from genetic research to shape interventions that will be more and more effective.

But it's worse than that. We don't get *excited* about psychosocial intervention the way we get giddy whenever DNA is mentioned. Psychosocial intervention is messy, takes a lot of time, and demands lots of resources, and only results in modest improvements. And it looks puny compared to the promise of genetic science and medicine. Genetic work will figure everything out, right? It will rewrite our diagnostic guidelines and lead to blood tests that will tell a parent if a kid has a particular disorder, right? It will lead to a cure that will make the disease go away, right? And it will even flag the disease before it starts and prevent it, right? Well, if genetic research led to those breakthroughs, who wouldn't be thrilled? I sure would. But we've been saying that for a long time now; in my career, I've heard these arguments about genetics for about 25 years. And guess what? Those disorders still exist, still impact lots of kids, and still demand better interventions.

I could go on and on about this. So perhaps it is more productive to raise questions I've heard lots of times – and even asked myself – and think about the answers.

AREN'T MAGIC BULLETS POSSIBLE?

Genetic research can be seductive – much more so than environmental approaches. If we can reduce the etiology of a disorder to the actions of a single gene, isn't it possible then to develop some type of biological intervention to correct for whatever that rogue gene is doing? Well, the amazing answer is yes! Although it sounds like science fiction to someone like me who does not work in a wet lab, there is proof of principle in this concept.

Back in 1960, the scientists Peter Nowell and David Hungerford identified a chromosomal abnormality – a translocation known as the Philadelphia chromosome – in which parts of two chromosomes (chromosomes 9 and 22) swap places. This creates a fusion gene on chromosome 22 (BCR on chromosome 22 joined with ABL from chromosome 9) that produces a protein (a tyrosine kinease) that speeds up cell division and also interferes with the DNA's ability to repair itself. The primary clinical result is the eventual onset of chronic myelogenous leukemia (CML), which is an uncontrolled proliferation of CML cells.

The amazing thing about the discovery of the Philadelphia chromosome is that in the late 1990s a drug was identified (imatinib or Gleevec/Glivec) that could inhibit the rapid growth and accumulation of the CML cells. Although this drug is not a cure for CML, it has proven to be remarkably effective in controlling the production of CML cells and thus permits people with the Philadelphia chromosome to lead healthy, disease-free lives.

SO AREN'T SIMILAR SUCCESSES IMMINENT?

Given the success of a targeted pharmacological intervention aimed at the Philadelphia chromosome, why shouldn't we expect more magic bullets? Why should we be cautious in assuming that we will eventually see similar breakthroughs for child and adolescent psychopathology since genetics is assumed to play such a crucial role in etiology? Won't we someday be able to prevent or cure autism spectrum disorder, attention deficit hyperactivity disorder, and depression?

First, note that it is particularly unwise to make predictions about the yield of genetic research. The science of genetics can change quickly and dramatically because of technology – what was state-of the-art yesterday can become passé tomorrow. So it would not surprise me to find out that, say, a chapter in this book becomes obsolete days after this work is published. It happens sometimes – and if it happens to lead to a dramatic improvement in our ability to intervene positively in children's lives, that would be great.

That said, there are a fair number of identified single-gene disorders, yet to date magic bullets have been elusive to find. There are countless examples. I'll briefly mention Huntington's disease (HD) because it is a neurological disorder and thus has some parallels with psychopathology in that the focus is on genes that are expressed in the brain. HD is caused by a genetic defect on chromosome 4. A part of DNA – called a CAG repeat expansion – occurs many more times than normal (it repeats 36 to 120 times as compared to 10 to 35 times). This gene is inherited. It is passed on from parent to child as a dominant gene so that if a parent has the gene, a child has a 50% chance of inheriting it (assuming the other parent does not have the gene). It can occur in multiple forms (for example, early vs. late onset), and can give rise to a variety of symptoms, but the eventual prognosis for all affected is neural degeneration and death due to the gene.

Although the identification of the genetic locus of this disease was a major achievement (and bear in mind the critical work was done in the 1980s), to date this has not been translated into an effective prevention or treatment. HD thus serves as an unfortunate reminder of the great challenges involved in moving from an identified genetic etiology to a successful targeted treatment. While research aimed at such an outcome will continue and certainly should be supported, it will be important to consider alternative interventions for genetic conditions in lieu of magic bullets as these have proven to be elusive.

Furthermore, besides being brilliant, the scientists who discovered the Philadelphia chromosome and the HD gene could make these discoveries because there was a specific rogue gene to be identified. For some disorders, single genes that have been identified convey a large statistical risk but they are not deterministic – just because you have the gene doesn't mean you will get the disorder, and you can get the disorder even if you don't have the gene.

One example of this principle is found in advances that identified genes involved in breast cancer. A mutation in one of two genes – BRCA1 and BRCA2 (so named as breast cancer susceptibility gene 1 and breast cancer susceptibility gene 2) – greatly increases the risk for breast cancer in women. About 60% of women who inherit a mutation in BRCA1 or BRCA2 will develop breast cancer at some point in their life, as compared to the population rate of 12%. While this is a very significant risk for women with one of these mutations, it is important to note that, unlike HD, this is a probabilistic rather than deterministic effect – about 40% of women will not get breast cancer even if they are at genetic risk. And to date, the ability to test for BRCA1 and BRCA2 provide women with complex decisions, including if they want to get tested, and how to interpret probabilities assigned to risk genes. Furthermore, the preventive option to date – ablation – is not a magic bullet but an invasive technique that women need to consider carefully.

Thus far, we have three take-away messages. First, even if the genetic locus for a single-gene disorder has been identified, the translation to intervention is clearly not an easy step. Second, the picture gets more complicated when identified genes aren't deterministic even if they have a large effect size. Third, these examples all derive from genetic findings that *predated* the HGP. Geneticists have been able, for a long time, to identify rare single-gene disorders. The gene for Huntington's disease was reported in the scientific literature in 1983. Such Mendelian disorders typically follow classic laws of genetics and scientific tools to detect them have been around for a long time.

This leads us to a fourth take-away message. There would be (I would think) consensus among geneticists that the vast majority of the disorders that concern us (including the common developmental, behavioral, and emotional disorders) are assumed to reflect the effects of not just one deterministic gene, or even one gene of large effect size, but rather the effects of many genes, each of which may represent a small piece of the puzzle. This is not a new thought. It's been the backbone of quantitative genetics for many decades. The principle was emphasized particularly in the 1990s when association studies that sought out the small effects of genes, and studies of specific candidate genes, became all the rage. But I think it was somewhat forgotten when our heads got turned by the HGP. Just because we could get our hands on all the genes doesn't mean they would start to behave differently than what we were thinking about them at the time. And any statistical geneticist could tell you, just from observing a pattern of inheritance in families, whether or not a single gene was "responsible" for a given disease – and they could do that way before the genes were identified. The tools to find those genes have been around for a relatively long period of time. As the ENCODE project is telling us, we are just starting to have a good look around the jungle to see how the genome really works.

WHAT WILL BE THE YIELD OF GENETIC RESEARCH IN TERMS OF INTERVENTION?

In some ways, the HGP is actually positioned to move science along to recognize and deal with this complexity. After all, if most disorders were assumed to reflect the combined effects of many genes, we'd need to be able to identify all of them in order to study how different genes come together to either protect someone from disease or make disease much more likely. Given this assumption, there are two related important concepts to keep in mind (throughout this book) when we are discussing the role of genes with respect to common childhood disorders: genomics and personalized medicine.

Most of the time, when we hear about advances in genetic research, there is reference to a particular gene. Think about the headlines you will see in the newspaper or when you look at your computer: "*Study shows gene W leads to disease Y.*" (Fill in whatever gene and disease you like.) In fact, what is typically happening is that studies are looking at the entire genome and identifying more and more genetic loci that are associated with risk for a disorder – but the magnitude of the association is much smaller than the headline would have you believe.

One of the key advances of the HGP has been to demonstrate convincingly that for most diseases we are talking about genomics rather than genetics. (For those of you with a little background in behavioral genetics, this is the post-genomic representation of quantitative genetics versus classical genetics.) Genomics deals with the effects of multiple genes, whereas genetics refers to the effects of a specific gene. Most common disorders are assumed to reflect the effects of many genetic loci, making genetic detection of risk a highly speculative – and complicated – venture. There is why the HGP was necessary and why it led the way for the gradual compilation of all the genes that could be involved in a particular disorder, with the latest iteration being the ENCODE project. For example, a recent paper suggests that, to date, 20 genetic loci have been identified for type 2 diabetes, 30 loci have been found for prostate cancer, and 18 loci have been associated with breast cancer.

That's the good news. The bad news is that it becomes a very messy picture to derive a "genetic risk" profile when you have a lot of genes in the mix. If you want to make your head spin, start to think of the statistical possibilities when there are lots of genetic loci involved. I'll get you started. Say there are 20 loci for a disorder. Assume that at each loci there are two types of alleles possible (labeled A and B). So at any one loci there are 3 possibilities (AA, AB, BB). That applies to each of the 20 loci. Now start to think of all the possible combinations you could come up with that could occur in an individual (while statistical geneticists can make this formulaic, it's worth your time to start to scribble it out and stay with it for 5 minutes like I do). Which of the possible combinations would indicate high genetic risk? Or, for that matter, low genetic risk?

One recent paper made a speculation that sounds very sensible. When you start to add up all the possibilities in the population, it may be that small proportions of individuals are at either low or high risk and most will be at some type of intermediate risk. This is where the second concept comes into play – personalized medicine. The idea is that by eventually putting together all the genetic pieces of the puzzle, we can get to the point where an individual could find out their "quantitative" genetic risk for a given disorder. I think this concept is actually a pretty realistic statement of how genes contribute to propensity for disorders. But there are big issues here. Will it really be possible to get to the point of identifying the finite number of genes that represent the spectrum of risk or protection for a given disorder? Even if that were the case, will it be feasible to draw up risk profiles that are meaningful, especially if most of the individuals in a population are at some type of moderate risk (by virtue of being human)?

Let's stay with this idea a bit longer. Imagine that this type of genomic profiling comes to fruition. Say at some point in the future you can take a given form of childhood psychopathology and generate a quantitative risk profile for kids. And let's assume that guidelines get developed that can provide an algorithm for defining high genetic risk (some concentration of genetic dosage that is associated with a high probability of developing the disorder). What would come next? As we've already seen, tracing the biological pathways of a single deterministic gene and coming up with a biological treatment tailored to that gene product has not been easy – so isn't it fair to assume that doing so when there are lots of genes involved will be harder? Wouldn't be even more difficult to think about developing differential biological treatments that get tailored to this quantitative soup of factorial combinations of a multitude of genomic indicators? Again, the point here is not to say that the science of genomics is flawed or should be dismissed; my goal is to show that we may need (especially in the here and now) to be much more skeptical that the knowledge gained will rapidly be translated into some of the promises that were made when the race to decode the human genome was in full stride.

WHERE WILL ALL OF THIS LEAD?

Let's get back to the clinical conditions that will be the focus of this book. Consider autism spectrum disorder, or reading disorder, or attention deficit hyperactivity disorder. Think about conduct disorder, drug abuse, and depression. Do we have specific genetic findings that have been translated into biological interventions that either treat these disorders or prevent them? No, we don't. So should we focus instead on the messy but potentially influential environmental interventions out there? Well, to a degree – and there are certainly scientists and clinicians and educators who do that day after day. But what's been happening in many areas of research is that the intervention perspective has embraced genomic research and folded some of the concepts into the services that can be offered to children and adolescents. In some cases, this has been explicit, and even put to the test using genetic markers. In other instances, it may appear to be more implicit, the product of accumulated wisdom drawn from many years of interdisciplinary study. And sometimes it may not even seem to connect the dots between genetics and environmental intervention – even though the case can be made for it.

This is the inspiration and the platform for this book. I'd like you to consider a somewhat eclectic mix of old and new ideas, straightforward and tangential arguments, and a compilation of ways in which genetic research has in fact either had an impact on how we might design better psychosocial interventions for developmental, behavioral, and emotional disorders – or how it could have such an influence if we sort through some ideas. This is a book that is more about big ideas that are emerging and novel approaches that illustrate potential ways forward – don't expect long, drawn out reviews of the literature! It's also a book that might challenge some perspectives here and there. And for good measure, it's a book that will dust off and shine up some rather well-established findings that have not received the amped up enthusiasm that is often reserved for genetic studies that may carry implications about how we treat a disorder 20 years from now. This is a book that focuses on what we can do right now to improve the lives of children and adolescents, using environmental designs, but combined with our growing sophistication about how genes have their influence. In some cases, we'll talk about "reprogramming" genetically influenced pathways via the environment. In other cases, we will explore how the effects of genes may be circumvented or shaped. Sometimes we will see that the environment has been given short shrift and attention to it may simply negate the impact of genes by making sure they never get activated. We will inevitably take on examples in which genes and environment seem to be inextricably linked, but in surprising ways that can direct new ways of thinking about changing the result of that mix via manipulation of the environment. So this book is about the future, but the immediate future in a kid's life. The spotlight will be turned brightly on a number of intriguing approaches by a variety of outstanding scientists who see the value of bringing together the study of nature and nurture to change what can be changed rather easily – the nurture part – in order to make the nature part work better.

CHAPTER

2

Autism Spectrum Disorder: Can We Use Environmental Intervention to Reprogram Genetic Effects?

Imagine that it is 2003. You have $1 million that you want to invest in research on autism spectrum disorder (ASD). You are trying to allocate this investment to have the most impact possible on changing the course of the disorder. You know that this goal is lofty, so you decide to temper it a bit. You focus on trying to find out what would be the most promising ways of altering fundamental mechanisms of brain functioning in kids with ASD in order to improve their social behavior.

To start, you recognize that ASD is, in essence, a brain disorder. You also understand that the brain dysfunction – whatever it may be – is primarily due to genetics. Indeed, you've heard many times that ASD is in fact a "genetic disorder." You do some reading and decide that identifying the genes that cause ASD can indicate how brain development is affected.

So you are thinking that this knowledge may lead to targeted biological interventions that could prevent ASD, eradicate it via things like tailored pharmacology, or at a minimum substantially alter the underlying brain dysfunction enough to improve the social development.

While this might have seemed like a pipe dream in the 1990s, you get excited because you agree that the Human Genome Project (HGP) might revolutionize diagnosis and therapeutics. If we have identified all the genes, we should have the tools to figure out what they do – and we should learn pretty quickly about the genes that affect brain development. We should also have the ability to then figure out which gene or genes cause ASD. Once we get that knowledge, we should be able to translate that information into therapeutics.

You also know (at this point in 2003) that ASD is believed to be one of the most heritable of the developmental disorders – in fact, one of the most heritable psychiatric disorders. A number of twin studies have been done suggesting that genes play a dominant role as a cause of ASD – and there is little evidence of environmental influence. So putting all the pieces together, you decide to invest that $1 million into genetic research, with the goal of developing a genetically informed biological treatment for ASD.

Now it's almost a decade later. You ask yourself – was that money well spent? You would answer, "Yes." There was nothing wrong with that strategy as executed in 2003. There would be nothing inherently wrong with that strategy right now. All of those basic goals are good ones, ones worth pursuing – and someday we might indeed see them pay off in a big way. But if you went through that exercise, right now as you are reading this, you might conclude that you should have invested only some of that $1 million into that program of genetic research. You might want to consider other avenues given your stated goal of being a catalyst for seeing changes in brain functioning that correspond to clinically significant and important improvements in social behavior.

In fact, you might consider investing at least half that amount – if not more – in psychosocial interventions. Part of the reason is that we've discovered new complexities about the genetics of ASD – some of which argue that we may have overestimated the importance of genes in the etiology of ASD, and some that illuminate how complex it may be to find genes or a set of genes that systematically represent the genetic architecture underlying the development of ASD. But part of the rationale is that we are also learning a great deal about the power of the environment – and specifically about the payoffs of labor-intensive and costly psychosocial intervention – to change aspects of brain functioning in ASD that have not yet been achieved via biological means. As you will see, the point is not just that intervention – any proactive intervention – is important (even though it is). We are starting to see evidence that the big changes we want to see – real, sustained, impactful improvements in social behavior mediated by neural processes – may be just as likely to arise via psychosocial intervention as opposed to biological strategies. And this is beginning to make sense given what we are learning about the genetics of ASD. This chapter will put all of these pieces together.

GENOMIC APPROACHES TO ASD

Understanding what a "genetic disorder" is and isn't can greatly affect our expectations about what we can, and can't, achieve via biology – or at least illuminate that this road may be a long and winding one for many years to come. In the classic sense, a genetic disorder is one that is caused, without exception, by a gene or genetic region. The genetic factor (whatever it is) is both necessary and sufficient to cause the disorder – necessary meaning that if it isn't present, the individual won't get the disorder, and sufficient meaning that if the individual does have the genetic factor, he or she will get the genetic disorder without the presence of any other risk factor. This is not new knowledge, but it's worth restating. There are many single-gene disorders, many of which are quite rare. They follow patterns of Mendelian inheritance that most high school students now learn in biology class. A good, detailed family history will reveal a pattern of inheritance consistent with Mendelian (single-gene) models – and suggest the likelihood of a dominant gene, or a recessive gene.

ASD is not inherited like a single-gene disorder. Genetic modeling – even before completion of the HGP – based on family history, would have indicated the likelihood of a single-gene etiology, as it did for Huntington's disease. However, this was not the case, as many individuals with ASD do not have parents with ASD – and many individuals with ASD do not have biological children. So the basic patterns of inheritance, just based on observing the distribution of the disorder within the family, would not be fully informative.

That said, it has also been suspected for decades that ASD appears to be heavily influenced by genes. Prior to the genomic revolution in science and the HGP, this viewpoint was shaped by the classic twin study. Identical (monozygotic or MZ) twins share all their genes; fraternal (dizygotic or DZ) twins only share, on average, half of their genes. If DNA fully explained a disorder, then MZ twins should show perfect concordance – if one twin is diagnosed with autism, the identical co-twin will be as well. Fraternal twins should be less similar overall – in this case, less concordant – since they only are "half similar" genetically. In twin studies, all of this can be summarized numerically with a heritability measure. Heritability can range from 0 (genes have no effect on, in the case, a disorder) to 1 (genes have a complete effect on the disorder in question).

The twin design can also tell us something about the impact of the environment, defined as nongenetic influence. The twin design can provide an estimate of how influential it is to be raised together, starting during the prenatal period. If exposure to similar environmental influences were important for ASD, this would in principle promote concordance between both MZ and DZ twins because it would not be impacted by genetic similarity. In this way, this type of environmental effect – which is called shared environment (it's duly noted some prefer the phrase common environment) – can also be modeled, and it too can range from 0 to 1.

Now, of course, lots of complexity can be (and has been) introduced into this type of statistical (or "biometrical") modeling. But we needn't get into that right now. Here's why. Most of the twin studies, performed from the late 1970s onward, came up with pretty much the same conclusion – the heritability of ASD was very high, and the shared environmental component was essentially 0. In some studies, the estimate of heritability was as high as .90. If you have a look at those scientific papers, you would see why. MZ twins were typically highly concordant, whereas DZ twins were not similar at all (in fact, most were discordant). All of this pointed to genes as a dominant etiological factor, with the environment having a negligible impact. In fact, this work was of historical importance, putting to rest (in the late 1970s) psychodynamic theories of ASD and helping to establish a mindset of ASD as a biological – and indeed genetic – disorder.

There was, however, one somewhat confusing aspect to these twin studies. As stated above, the DZ concordance rate was extremely low – indeed much lower than would be expected for a disorder with a strongly genetic etiology. After all, since DZ twins share, on average, half of their genes, shouldn't they be more similar? At the time, the speculation was that there may be a particular type of genetic effect happening in the case of ASD. For example, if there were only a few genes carrying the impact on the disorder, and if those genes had a synergistic (or interactive) effect, then the pattern of twin concordances could make sense (since MZ twins would be much more similar for these kind of "nonadditive genetic effects" as compared to DZ twins). And that seemed to make sense, except for one other lingering issue. Other studies focused on the biological siblings of children with ASD to evaluate their level of risk for ASD. From the genetic perspective, they were just like DZ twins – DZ twins are full biological siblings who are conceived and born at the same time. The biological siblings were unlike DZ twins since they did not share, in biological time, the same environmental influences (they were conceived and born at different times). So you'd think they would be even less similar than DZ twins. But they weren't – they were more similar with respect to concordance rates. Not nearly as similar as MZ twins, but they had significant concordance rates nonetheless.

Now, at this point, you might think that this type of ambiguity is irrelevant. The twin study may seem somewhat "old school" or outdated in the post-HGP era. No actual genes are identified or specified in the basic model – rather, the "net effect" of DNA is described using a somewhat peculiar (though arguably useful) metric. (In the most traditional model, environmental factors are not specified either.) Heritability is simply a descriptive statistic – it doesn't have a true "biological" meaning and was used primarily as a first step to determine if genetic strategies would be justified. So why bother getting into all this if the net result is simply gaining a bit more precision in the estimate of genetic effects on autism? The answer is that a new twin study published in 2011 – in fact, the largest twin study to date, using the most modern diagnostic criteria and methods to ascertain diagnoses – had very different findings that may serve to be a game-changer in the way we think about genes and autism. Here's why.

IS THERE A NEW FUNDAMENTAL ETIOLOGICAL MODEL OF ASD?

The key contribution of this new twin study (see Hallmayer et al., 2011) was twofold – it not only suggested that shared environmental factors were a major source of influence on ASD, they were in fact more influential in magnitude than the genetic effects. To be specific, shared environment was estimated to be 0.55, whereas the heritability was calculated at 0.37.

Now, of course, these are statistical estimates and they have a confidence interval around them. The headline, though, is that the most modern, largest twin study to date reported that twin similarity for autism was more strongly attributable to sharing a common environment than common genes. Or put another way – it's possible that, for a long time now, we've been overestimating the net genetic impact on ASD. To be clear, the study supports that genes are part of the equation in terms of risk for autism – but they are not the only variable in that equation, and the shared environmental term that we've thought was nil may in fact be pronounced.

Since this study is potentially revolutionary in recasting the magnitude of genetic influence on ASD – as well as the importance of the environment – it's worth going into why these results deviated from all those reported in the past. Part of the reason may simply be the larger sample size. Conducting a twin study is not especially easy because, while twins are not uncommon, it's still laborious to generate a large sample of MZ and DZ twins because they are not exactly common. The same goes for ASD – even though the rates are now thought to be very high in the population (1 in 110), again the pure numbers make doing a study with a larger sample size more difficult. Here, of course, you'd need to cross two factors in the study that make the study population difficult to identify – you would need twins, with at least one twin with ASD. Why is all this important? Simply put, since heritability is a descriptive statistic, it is sensitive to the sample size. The same goes for shared environment. The larger the sample, the better our estimate will be. In past studies, there have been very small samples of twins with autism. This current study was not huge by modern standards – 192 twin pairs were ascertained – but the study is very large given the restrictions of studying twins with ASD. So it may simply be that the prior studies simply underestimated concordance rates in DZ twins as a matter of chance and sampling estimation due to the small sample sizes.

It's also worth considering that this sample of 192 twins was community-based (drawn from a registry in the state of California). It was, in this sense, a representative sample in that there wasn't some obvious type of sampling bias that would skew the results. This makes us give more attention to these findings and take them even more seriously. In addition, it should be noted that this project used both a "strict" definition of autism, and a "broader" definition of ASD. The findings were essentially the same. All in all, the results were particularly clear and compelling – shared environmental factors matter, and using the language and metric of the twin study, matter even more than genetic factors.

At this point, it may seem like research has been misguided for a number of years. That's not it at all. Twin studies have been very valuable, despite the fact that they are natural experiments and limited in what they can tell us. They've played a key role over the past few decades in shaping our thinking on ASD. And even though we have seen the completion of the HGP, they continue to advance our knowledge. This particular twin study suggests that autism is, like many disorders, a "complex" disorder with respect to etiology – meaning simply that there is a mix of genetic and environmental influences that come together in some type of unspecified and undoubtedly complex way. What it tells us is that the idea of finding one or two or three genes for ASD that (whether together or separately) are the necessary and sufficient "causes" is highly unlikely. It means the story about what causes autism is likely going to be muddy and murky. It's going to be similar to the story for countless other "common" disorders – not just developmental ones but including cardiovascular diseases and many forms of cancer – that epidemiologists have classified as "complex" for decades. And it suggests we need to revisit our goals for genetic research on ASD, what it will tell us, and what we will do with it.

GENOMICS, COMPLEX DISORDERS, HYPE, AND HOPE

As discussed in Chapter 1, any reputable geneticist – whether biological or statistical in focus – would acknowledge that, relative to the initial claims surrounding the HGP, we have yet to develop tailored and impactful biological interventions for many (and in fact the majority) complex disorders based on genomic findings. There just aren't many big findings to report. Not just for ASD – for any complex disorder. Any major advances in therapeutics that have been guided by genetic findings have come via application to genetic disorders that have identifiable major gene effects on risk. There may be some exceptions – such as in oncology – but for the most part we are where we were before the completion of the HGP in terms of translation into treatment, or personalized intervention based on DNA.

This observation – one that has been made by many prominent players in the field of genomics – suggests that we need to recalibrate and reconsider exactly what we are learning from the work done over the last decade. We need to think about what the lack of rapid translation into therapeutics is telling us. With complex disorders like ASD, we need to reflect on what the rational and realistic expectations should be for the current generations of individuals who suffer from this condition.

It seems that magic bullets from genomics are not on the immediate horizon. Again, if they happen – terrific! Let's apply them. But we have to stop thinking that magic bullets are a given. We need to refrain from assuming that genomics is going to be our big gun in this etiological fight. And, it will be argued, we need to start thinking more out of the box on how we might be able to apply knowledge gleaned from the whole range of genetically informative studies (twin studies, molecular studies) to develop better, more impactful, and more lasting interventions.

To this end, it's worth stepping back and considering what has been happening on the genomic side with ASD. There has been, and continues to be, an intriguing trail of clues about the genetics of autism – without major findings in the sense of establishing a genetic etiology. This certainly reinforces the idea that autism is in fact a complex disorder and will not be easily explained by a major genetic effect. Much effort has been put into developing large collaborative efforts with informative samples that would provide a platform for the complexities of doing searches for genes involved in risk for autism. What is the big picture that has emerged from this work? Well, there are actually two big pictures.

One study indicates that there are a number of potential genes that have been associated with autism. How many? One study suggested that genetic markers from 146 genes (representing 247 single-nucleotide polymorphisms or SNPs) can be combined in a quantitative model to generate a pretty good prediction of a diagnosis of ASD (Skafidas et al., 2012). Bear in mind that this work is preliminary and it is not being used in any type of clinical manner right now. It may be that we are still in the earliest stages of exploring the genetics of autism as a complex disorder with many genes assumed to play a role – with lots of potential markers that have been identified. Current thinking also focuses on potential interactions between some of the genetic loci. All of this is complex stuff, and in tune with the presumed tangle of multiple genetic influences that come together in elusive ways to contribute to risk for ASD. Bioinformatic approaches continue to be developed to deal with the mind-boggling computational demands presented by the arrays of genetic markers that need to be considered. But to the point of this chapter, it should be appreciated that the genomic side of ASD supports the notion that translation of these findings – even if they mature in the near future – will be a slippery proposition. This is especially so since we don't even have, as of now, a good model for how this will happen with any complex disorder.

As noted above, there is a second big picture that's come out of the work to date on the genetics of autism. In contrast to the approach of trying to identify a multitude of genes (or, in the parlance of genomics, common variants) that would constitute the basis for polygenic inheritance (meaning lots of genes), a different tactic has gained some traction. This alternate model has reported a number of mutations ("rare and de novo copy-number variants" – see, for example, Huguet, Ey, & Bourgeron, 2013) in some individuals with ASD. Similar to the polygenic approach, over 100 different genetic loci have been reported to date (and counting). Unlike the polygenic approach, these findings have differed greatly from individual to individual. It's like, in some of these studies, each individual with ASD may have their own unique genetic mutation that may contribute to etiology. There is speculation that some of these mutations ("spontaneous mutations") may originate with fathers, be correlated with paternal age at conception, and passed down like an inherited gene. Now, on the one hand, this might make you think that this approach takes us back to the focus on single or major genes. Perhaps it does – but it may only apply to a small number of cases of ASD in the population. There are of course other genetic conditions – such as Fragile X syndrome and Rett syndrome – which lead to symptoms consistent with ASD. It's just not clear, though, if this line of work is going to lead to breakthroughs that will apply to the vast majority of individuals with ASD. In the field, scientists will discuss this as "genetic heterogeneity" – there may be a number of "classes" of etiological models of ASD that apply differentially to only some cases, and not others. And it is certainly hard to fathom, from the perspective of translation to treatment, how we will handle hundreds (or more) of unique mutations that may be associated with only a handful of cases – although the possibility that fundamental gene–brain development pathways should be entertained (but not assumed).

At this point, it looks like there is convergence between the recent twin study and the last decade or so of genomic research on autism. We haven't even begun to think about the implications of the new ENCODE perspective (discussed in the Preface), which argues that all of these identified regions of DNA that might be implicated in ASD can be under the orchestration of many other regions on DNA. And let's not forget the big take-home message of the twin study – that the environment matters too, and perhaps in a very big way. All of this implies that tailored and personalized interventions based on genomics will be really elusive. However, that does not mean that we aren't seeing progress in altering the developmental trajectories of youth with ASD.

USING THE ENVIRONMENT TO REPROGRAM THE EFFECTS OF GENES

The somewhat messy findings from the genetic studies of ASD should not be confused as a lack of progress. All of the intensive effort is giving us a very realistic picture of where we are at and where we want to be, which is much more informative than the hope and hype that surrounded the HGP. That's part of what research does – it illuminates what we don't know and the challenges that await us. But there's more. The idea that there are all kinds of genetic risk factors contributing to ASD, along with a host of unidentified environmental influences, suggests that there may be room for plasticity within all of this complexity. If there is some type of "perfect storm" involving a number of collisions of genetic and environmental risk that play out in the prenatal and postnatal periods, and continue through infancy and toddlerhood and childhood, can we be somewhat optimistic that there is at least some window of opportunity to interfere with this process and reshape development? Can we think about the end products of these gene, gene–gene, and gene–environment effects and devise ways of using the environment to shape direction in normative ways? Could we even think of environmentally "reprogramming" the net impact of genes? Recent work suggests that this is not only a possibility, but in fact may be unfolding in a tangible way (again, something that can't be said for biologically tailored interventions).

Many geneticists have suggested – and continue to contend – that the real progress from genomic research will come not from identifying genes, but from gaining insight into how these genes may converge to shape biological processes and patterns of brain development. Such gene–brain-behavior links have been a staple in thinking about the etiology of complex psychiatric disorders for a long time – but the ideas may be gaining traction because of the new insights gleaned from genomics. Maybe the pathology underlying autism is not so much about the immediate biological products of specific genes, but rather in the orchestration of brain development that is influenced by genetic convergence and environmental impact. This could play out at the cellular (e.g., synaptic) level, the organizational (anatomical) level, or a functional level. But the idea is that if there is the complex, dynamic interplay going on developmentally (rather than just some type of genetic determinism), we just might be able to think about how the psychosocial environment can be added to this mix in a therapeutic way.

Here's where the new thinking with respect to ASD is providing the most exciting lead we've had on coming up with tailored interventions. When we think of a tailored intervention, we can consider programs that are geared to a particular individual with a given profile (e.g., some type of genetic marker that is highly informative). But we can also entertain the idea that interventions can be tailored to the assumed "end points" of genetic influence and the confluence with environmental factors. The idea here would be that we've learned quite a bit – perhaps primarily from twin studies and family studies – about the nature and boundaries of the ASD phenotype that is impacted in part by genes. We know this involves some variation in brain development that makes the social world not very inviting, attractive, or the target of attention in babies and toddlers who are developing ASD. The smiles, laughs, and voices in the social world don't hold the allure they do in normally developing babies and toddlers. But is this developmental trajectory fixed?

Geraldine Dawson, Sally Rogers, and colleagues have created a psychosocial intervention that assumes there is the potential for plasticity in this mix (see Rogers et al., 2012). They have been clearly and cleverly thinking about gene–environment interplay when designing the pioneering Early Start Denver Model (ESDM). Prior to the development of the ESDM, psychosocial interventions aimed at ASD relied on techniques derived from learning models to try to shape appropriate behaviors in youth with autism. Of particular note is Applied Behavior Analysis (ABA), which is a generic (in the sense that it is not specific to autism) intervention that uses principles of reinforcement to bring about positive changes in behavior. For example, with toddlers, target behaviors such as looking, listening, and conversing (in a logical way as in conversation) can be rewarded in intensive training sessions, with the idea that they will generalize and become part of a child's behavioral repertoire.

ABA has certainly proved to be effective in children, teens, and adults with autism. It helps to promote basic life skills as well as reduce some of the social and communicative deficits associated with autism. But the innovation of the ESDM was to use the basic learning principles of ABA – and their known efficacy – and expand them into a comprehensive developmental intervention that is directly tailored to the social and communicative deficits that underlie autism and undoubtedly reflect the end product expression of the intersection of putative risk genes and environmental factors. The key to all of this is to postulate that if an intervention can engage a child with ASD with their social environment, continued engagement might stimulate plasticity and "reprogram" the brain to process social stimuli in a more proactive way and hence promote more social behavior. You can think of this as reprogramming the brain to override the genetic signals that don't react to social stimuli and become conditioned to selectively attend and process all the rich information that is out there in the social world – and to generate neural connections that promote social responses that are not, if you will, "in the genes." Since genetic influences are, in the emerging models, somewhat malleable and sensitive to the environment (in a negative way), perhaps the genetically shaped neural pathways can also be induced to respond in a positive way. Consider this perspective offered by Dawson and colleagues in one of their recent papers (Dawson et al., 2012):

> Of interest is whether and how early intervention alters the trajectory of brain development. The development of social and language brain circuitry – its acquisition, organization, and function – results from an interaction between a young child and his or her social environment. During reciprocal social interaction, engagement with a

> social partner facilitates the cortical specialization of perceptual and representational systems for social and linguistic information. Therefore, the early lack of social engagement associated with ASD could have negative secondary effects on behavioral and brain development. Early intervention that is designed to enhance social attention and affective and social engagement, thereby promoting the development of cognitive and language skills, may serve to alter a child's brain development toward a more normal developmental trajectory.

How does ESDM work? There are a number of core features, including:

- A focus on positive affect and interpersonal exchanges
- Emphasis on shared engagement with joint activities
- Using affect-based relationship dynamics to teach language and communication skills

ESDM is intensive. It typically involves considerable dedication and effort by parents along with highly trained therapists. In some of the published studies therapists offer intervention for 2 hours, twice a day, 5 days a week – for 2 years. That's right, 2 years. Parents use the ESDM strategies during the course of daily life. This is a substantial effort all the way around. It is demanding because it is designed to be naturalistic – the training and learning happens in the stream of real-world interaction. This is a key factor because this is part of the genetic "liability" of autism. There is a lack of motivation for spontaneous social interaction in autism. Designing an intervention that is intended to happen within a naturalistic context takes this on directly and bodes well for generalization (or "reprogramming"). There is also training in specific behaviors, such as face recognition.

There are two extremely important findings to report. The first is that the evidence to date suggests that ESDM has benefits for toddlers with autism. Dawson, Rogers, and colleagues conducted a controlled randomized trial (2010) that compared ESDM with community intervention (CI) – a stringent test in that it is expected that CI would also confer some therapeutic advantage. CI did have an effect – about half a standard deviation's worth – on a range of outcome measures (including IQ testing, language skills, adaptive behavior, and diagnostic status at the study's end). However, the ESDM group improved by more than a standard deviation on these outcomes – clear evidence of efficacy.

With respect to the themes of this chapter, a recent follow-up study provided striking results that help to account for the efficacy of ESDM – this form of intervention normalized the brain activity of toddlers after the 2 years of application (Dawson et al., 2012). Dawson, Rogers and collaborators took electroencephalography (EEG) readings of the electrical activity of the children with autism when they were looking at toys and when they were looking at faces. Prior work has established that, in children with autism, the brain is more highly activated when they are looking at a toy (an inanimate object) as compared to a face – and that the opposite is the case for normally developing children (who show more brain activity in response to a face). In this study, the children who were given ESDM showed the normal preference for a face versus a toy, as validated by brain activity, whereas those who had received CI did not. In fact, their patterns of brain activity were indistinguishable from a group of normally developing youth who were matched for age.

Let's reflect on these accumulating findings. They are stunning, and arguably the first time that we've seen evidence of any intervention – psychosocial or biological – having some type of normalizing effect on the brain functioning of youth with ASD. While ESDM is not a "cure" for ASD, it is an intervention that offers evidence of real change. It provides proof of principle that developmental trajectories that are assumed to be under the strong control of risk genes and toxic environmental effects may nonetheless show signs of plasticity. Indeed, core features of the syndrome of ASD – those that any genetic theory of ASD would postulate as being phenotypic end products of genetic influence – are now being shown to be reactive to psychosocial intervention. All of this is quite remarkable, especially if you have ever spent time with a child with autism.

Let me expand briefly on that point. When I was in graduate school, one of the questions on my qualifying exam asked us to talk about the concept of plasticity, and explain how it is useful as a general principle of development. I wasn't trying to be clever in my response, but rather honest, based on about seven years of experience of working with kids with ASD. I used ASD to illustrate that, at that moment in history, you couldn't just throw around the term *plasticity*. In my experience, children with ASD showed very little in the way of plasticity. Interventions were helpful but only in the moment – when you took them away, the core autistic behaviors returned. And I argued that, at a neural level, there would be no real evidence of change in processing social stimuli or reacting in a different manner in social situations. Until those conditions could be met, I just didn't see how plasticity applied to ASD. Although we are still in the early stages of research on ESDM, if I were answering that question today, my answer would be quite different.

WHAT'S NEXT?

Where do we stand now with respect to ASD? How does all of this come together in terms of genetics and intervention?

First, it may be speculated that if we had in the literature a new study that showed a change in brain activity in children with ASD based on a biological intervention – particularly if it was tailored via a candidate gene – it would be a very big deal in the popular press. In fact, it would be a much bigger deal than showing how the ESDM can influence brain functioning. Why? Because we still all buy into the idea that biological intervention implies "cures," whereas psychosocial interventions suggest that we are doing what we can until we have a cure. The thing is, unfortunately, we don't know that we'll ever have a cure for ASD – just like we may never have cures for heart disease or diabetes or other common and complex diseases. We may have to settle, perhaps for a very long time, for interventions that simply make functioning better and development more normalized.

Second, we do not have any true evidence that genetic research on ASD is going to produce biological indicators that will help tailor intervention. We like to think that we will – and if we don't, it won't be because of a lack of effort or talent. We have many very gifted scientists devoting their life to this. The issue is that, for the complex diseases, we just don't know what the yield of genomic science will be respective to translational efforts. This is a moving target, and the game keeps changing as we learn more and more how complex genomics really is and will continue to be.

This leads to the third point – we now have some evidence that tailored early intervention efforts might have an impact on ASD. It might normalize some behaviors, and maybe it's in part reprogramming the brain to avoid the consequences of those genetic signals that underlie autism. This kind of tailoring – focusing specific interventions on the core aspects of a complex disorder that have been shown, over and over again, to represent the phenotypic expression of the presumed underlying genetic liability – is novel and pragmatic in the sense that it can be tried right now. And we are seeing some intriguing evidence that it might be a very productive avenue to follow.

This kind of work, however, is not easy. It's labor intensive and costly. Think about the level of effort that goes into ESDM. Add up the hours over a 2-year period and the dedication of the families and therapists and the children with ASD. Going back to the hypothesis posed at the beginning of this chapter, this is why you might now want to endorse investing at least half of that $1 million to psychosocial research efforts if the goal is to achieve a meaningful clinical change in a population that suffers from a disorder that is influenced by genes. We put a lot of money into genetic research. It's been dominant in a very tangible way over the last decade. You can see it at the level of funding agencies – and know how enticed they get by genetic studies, and how lukewarm they can be toward intervention. Biology rules. Magic bullets aren't psychosocial in origin. And the big bang will come in the wet lab – not in the day-to-day interaction of a child with ASD and a parent. Or will it?

So what's next? Psychosocial interventions like ESDM are a necessary part of the future, and perhaps the most powerful approach we will have. But it can be sharpened – particularly if it continues to be informed and guided by genetically informative research. For example, ESDM is particularly effective with children who have a mild form of ASD. It may not translate as well to toddlers who show more severe levels of impairment including more cognitive dysfunction. Is there a genetic basis for this? Will identifying genes that underlie genetic heterogeneity give some clue about whether or not ESDM will be effective for some toddlers and not others – and will that process help explain why? Is it the case, for example, that cases of ASD linked to rare mutations show a worse developmental course as opposed to those who do not have identifiable mutations (and thus perhaps have some density of risk genes)? Will we learn about other neural processes, driven by that complex interplay between genes and environment, that could lead to modifications of ESDM that will make it more effective? Is it time to start thinking about more creative and forward looking ways of connecting what goes on in the wet lab with what happens in the social environment, particularly when a promising intervention is being put into place? Nobody has a crystal ball that tells us exactly which way we need to go for the immediate future, and for the more distant future. But dividing up the available resources in a way that merges genomic research with psychosocial intervention could provide synergistic dividends capable of changing the lives of many children – not in principle, but in practice.

REFERENCES

Dawson, G., Jones, E. J., Merkel, K., Venema, K., Lowy, R., Faja, S., Kamara, D., Murias, M., Greenson, J., Winter, J., Smith, M., Rogers, S. J., & Webb, S. J. (2012). Early behavioral intervention is associated with normalized brain activity in young children with autism. *Journal of the American Academy of Child and Adolescent Psychiatry*, *51*, 1150–1159.

Dawson, G., Rogers, S. J., Munson, J., Smith, M., Winter, J., Greenson, J., Donaldson, A., & Varley, J. (2010). Randomized, controlled trial for an intervention for toddlers with autism: The Early Start Denver Model. *Pediatrics*, *125*, e17–23.

Hallmayer, A., Cleveland, S., Torres, A., Phillips, A., Cohen, B., Torigoe, G., Miller, J., Fedele, A., Collins, J., Smith, K., Lotspeich, L., Croen, L. A., Ozonoff, S., Lajonchere, C., Grether, J. K., & Risch, N. (2011). Genetic heritability and shared environmental factors among twin pairs with autism. *Archives of General Psychiatry*, 68, 1095–1102.

Huguet, G., Ey, E., & Bourgeron, T. (2013). The genetic landscapes of autism spectrum disorders. *Annual Review of Genomics and Human Genetics*, *14*, 191–213.

Rogers, S. J., Estes, A., Lord, C., Vismara, L., Winter, J., Fitzpatrick, A., Guo, M., & Dawson, G. (2012). Effects of a brief Early Start Denver Model (ESDM)-based parent intervention on toddlers at risk for autism spectrum disorders: A randomized controlled trial. *Journal of the American Academy of Child and Adolescent Psychiatry*, *51*, 1052–1065.

Skafidas, E., Testa, R., Zantomio, D., Chana, G., Everall, I. P., & Pantells, C. (2014). Predicting the diagnosis of autism spectrum disorder with gene pathway analysis. *Molecular Psychiatry*, *19*, 504–510.

CHAPTER

3

Attention-Deficit/Hyperactivity Disorder and Reading Disorder: Illuminating How the Environment Shapes Highly Heritable Disorders

ADHD (attention-deficit/hyperactivity disorder) is one of the most highly heritable disorders that emerge in childhood. There are decades of twin studies that all converge on extremely high heritability estimates – typically quoted as being somewhere between 70% and 90% (see Thapar, Cooper, Eyre, & Langley, 2013). In some studies the heritability might be calculated to be nearly as high as that for height. Reading disorder (RD) also has a robust heritability, though not as high as ADHD. While the typical range reported in most reviews is between 40% and 60%, certain components of RD can yield heritability estimates in excess of 70%. For both disorders, all studies using genetically informative designs (both twin and adoption paradigms) converge on the conclusion that genes play a primary etiological role. In addition, because ADHD and RD co-occur, many genetic models postulate overlapping etiological influences that promotes risk for both disorders and their comorbid presentation.

Part of the progress in disseminating knowledge about these disorders has been to reinforce the idea that they are genetically influenced conditions. Prior generations often described kids with ADHD as just being lazy or lacking discipline. If you read descriptions of ADHD written for the lay public now, they often talk about ADHD not being due to laziness, or bad parenting, or a lack of discipline. They emphasize that ADHD is a biological disorder – and the driving force of the biology is rooted in the genome. A parallel approach can be discerned with RD. Decades ago kids with RD may have been labeled as being "slow" in a way that underestimated their overall level of cognitive ability and overgeneralized the sometimes very specific neuropsychological issues they experience. "Laziness" may have also entered the discussion. So the idea that genes may "cause" both ADHD and RD has been important for dispensing with derogatory and incorrect notions about these disorders. The idea is that both kids described above would be recognized as having a problem that requires intervention – and that the problem has genetic roots.

But the story about ADHD and RD is not as straightforward as this. The heritability data are compelling and from a computational point of view not disputed. But as we will see, these data do not necessarily indicate that we should treat ADHD and RD as primarily genetic disorders with no shaping from the environment. While there are hints of specific genes being linked with ADHD and/or RD, it's clear that we don't have formal genetic models and known causative genes – perhaps suggesting that we need to revisit our thinking on how genes work for these disorders. We are certainly not at a point where genetic tests can be used for diagnostic screening for either RD or ADHD – particularly as these disorders are inherently dimensional (without clear-cut guidelines for empirically justified cutoff points) and the expression of symptoms may in fact be reactive to various environmental influences. And there are no interventions that are tailored to specific genetic findings for either ADHD or RD.

There is a current of thinking in the field about the underrated role that environmental influences may play by intersecting with genes in a number of ways to shape how ADHD and RD manifest in real-world contexts. Such a vision may have profound implications for how we think about the need for new ways of incorporating – and evaluating – psychosocial interventions that may help improve the developmental trajectories for kids with ADHD and/or RD. And as we will see, there may be many questions about the environment that we may want to ask if we would get our best traction on what sets apart those two kids described above from other kids who aren't struggling in a classroom.

GENETIC MODELS OF ADHD AND RD: WHY HAS GENE DISCOVERY BEEN SO ELUSIVE?

It makes sense to discuss ADHD and RD together. As noted earlier, they are highly comorbid conditions – so a good number of genetic studies have examined both disorders. ADHD and

RD may be thought of in part as disorders that involve dysfunctions in basic cognitive functions (like directing and sustaining attention, processing words, etc.). ADHD and RD often get diagnosed in the early years of secondary school. The typical window for ADHD has been around age 7 (although the idea of diagnosing ADHD at younger ages will be discussed) – such as when kids are in 1st grade. The possibility of RD generally arises a little later in development (corresponding to expectations about when reading ability matures) and often becomes a diagnostic option after 2nd grade. It is clear that ADHD and RD can have profound negative influences on a child's development. Untreated, both can lead to low self-esteem, difficulties forming friendships, school failure, and a corresponding cascade of risk for later behavioral problems and substance use. Perhaps most importantly, it is believed that there are common etiological influences on both (including genetic contributions) along with risk factors that are specific to each disorder.

As noted above, ADHD and RD have been studied using behavioral genetic methods and have been shown to be highly heritable across many studies. While heritability estimates are just that – they are statistical representations of how influential genes might be in explaining why individuals differ – let's consider for a moment the implications of findings to date. The studies suggest that ADHD is primarily due to genes. There is little evidence in the model that the environment has much of an impact. So we would anticipate that if there were genes to be found, molecular geneticists would find them. Yet there are few replicated, established genetic loci that have been shown to be causes of ADHD and RD – in the way that we think about causation for genetic disorders. That is sobering news given the level of research effort to date, especially a decade past the completion of the Human Genome Project (HGP).

Why has the search for specific genes been so elusive? Let's begin with what we believe to be the most appropriate – meaning empirically supported – genetic model. Without exception, the prevailing opinion is that many genes, each of which has a small effect size, influence both ADHD and RD. The genetically informative studies to date – primarily twin studies but other variants including adoption designs – yield findings that conform well to the additive genetic model that assumes many genes of small effect size all add up in a quantitative way to have a total impact on development. Keep in mind that if ADHD or RD were due to a single gene, or even a major gene that had a profound influence on the disorder, we would be able to see that in these research designs – as well as family studies that combine information from multiple generations. The process of isolating genes with small effect sizes is painstaking despite the advances in technology that have occurred in genetics over the last few decades. Because each gene provides a low "signal," it is difficult to know with certainty that it has been discovered in all the "noise." Very large samples are required. Results need to be replicated. Different strategies are employed and evaluated. For example, the candidate gene approach has been used with ADHD, with a focus on genes involved in the regulation of the neurotransmitter dopamine. Dopamine is of interest because the drugs used to treat ADHD influence dopaminergic activity in the brain. Some dopaminergic genes have been found to be associated with ADHD – but not to the point where we know for certain that they play a key role in etiology.

Another approach uses a case-control framework (e.g., get a group of kids with RD, and another group without RD) to examine the whole genome in one big quantitative shot. For RD, some genes have shown to be of interest – but again with caveats and limitations surrounding the inferences that can be made.

So despite the strong evidence that genes play a "primary" role for both ADHD and RD, it's no simple task to identify all the genes involved for the disorders as defined using the standard diagnostic criteria. It will be a slow process. There will be positive findings that don't get replicated. Putting all the slowly emerging genetic pieces together is going to be complicated in a quantitative sense – for example, will kids be given a genetic "score" that indicates risk for ADHD? Is this effort worth pursuing? Yes. But is it clear that it will result in all the information we need to gather in order to more accurately diagnose these disorders and devise targeted effective interventions that will radically alter the trajectory of the two hypothetical case studies offered at the beginning of this chapter? No. Not until we see clear examples of "additive genetic" disorders in which a majority of genes are identified and that information is shown to give sufficient insight into the underlying biological processes to permit the development of tailored interventions that offer more improvement than the treatments currently available.

What strategies could be considered given the complexity of deciphering a number of unspecified genes that each carry only a small risk for a disorder? Historically, much effort has been devoted to endophenotypes, or underlying indicators of genetic risk that gets translated in developmental time in clinical phenotypes. For example, ADHD and RD could be broken down into fundamental neurocognitive processes that might better reflect the genetic signaling. While many endophenotypes have been considered and some may show promise (such as slow processing speed), again there are no concrete findings that have illuminated specific genes. The field continues to search for the "perfect phenotype" that will yield more easily to genetic methods (Skiba, Landi, Wagner, & Grigorenko, 2011).

WHY WOULD THE ENVIRONMENT BE IMPORTANT FOR HIGHLY HERITABLE DISORDERS?

If disorders like ADHD and RD are primarily heritable, shouldn't quantitative and molecular genetics be our only paths to follow, since the studies published to date show little evidence of environmental influence? While there is a reality to saying that we need to continue to search for these elusive risk genes, it isn't the case that no other strategies are warranted – or that the environment doesn't make a difference. Quantitative genetic methods provide statistical representations that reflect the "what is" rather than the "what could be" in a population. Heritability is a descriptive statistic that gives us a handle on how important genes may be when particular populations are studied at specific times using defined measurements and methods. It doesn't reflect a literal representation of how many genes are involved or in fact how much explanatory power we will have if we identify all the genes. This is not a new perspective and in fact is embedded into quantitative genetic theory. But it's important to make the implication of this point more transparent when we are talking about complex disorders like ADHD and RD where the actual structure of the phenotype can be questioned, and as we reflect on what the deliverable of gene identification will be for complex traits and disorders.

Cross-cultural research on RD can shed light on how gene expression into clinical phenotypes can vary based on a range of contextual factors. Individuals with RD can be identified all over the world. There have been studies that show how the core phenotype can be found in multiple cultures. But the rates of RD can, and do, vary widely by culture. For example, the rate of dyslexia in the United States and England is about twice as high as what is found in Italy. If we were to think of RD as a genetic disorder, we might be tempted to think that ethnic differences in genes would be the root of these differences. Such ethnic differences in gene variants can play a large role in risk for disease, and as such wouldn't be out of the question.

But the genetic explanation wouldn't take us very far. The reason for the cultural variation in rates of RD is the technical structure of the language. Some languages – like Italian – have a high degree of convergence between how words are spelled and how they sound. The rules linking words and their pronunciation are straightforward. Other languages – like English – pose more challenges. The ways in which words are spelled don't link up so cleanly with how they sound. There are many unusual rules and exceptions to the rules.

So the thinking is that there is an underlying genetic vulnerability to RD that gets expressed to varying degrees depending on the type of language being learned. In this case the quantitative genetic model of liability – introduced formally in the literature in the 1960s – can explain why we observe such cultural differences. The liability model posits that there are a number of genes that add up to represent an aggregate level of risk for a disorder (this is the additive genetic model introduced earlier). Genetic liability to a disorder gets expressed differentially (e.g., a clinically meaningful profile versus one that does not meet diagnostic criteria) depending on nongenetic factors. Conceptually, this model can be used as a heuristic to think about a given individual's level of risk for a disorder. Each person may have a certain number of the additive gene variants that reflect risk for the disorder. Depending on the density of these variants (e.g., how many they have), they are at more or less prone to get the disorder. This person may also experience nongenetic events or triggers that increase the risk for the disorder. As these etiological forces add up, they push an individual closer and closer to manifesting the symptoms. The genotype gets expressed as a disorder only when the nongenetic factors provide the extra dosage of risk to the underlying vulnerability.

This kind of model can be applied to RD. There may be an underlying spectrum of liability or propensity for RD. When the language is straightforward from a technical point of view, higher levels of genetic "loading" would be required to elicit symptoms of RD. Lower doses would not impact reading ability as much because the brain could handle the demands. If the language is more complex, however, even lower doses of genetic risk could get translated into RD because the stress on the processing system would be more challenged.

The larger point here is that the risk genotypes for complex disorders like RD and ADHD get expressed differentially depending on the context. To make it more concrete, consider a pair of identical twins that are born in the United States but separated at birth. One twin remains in the United States, and one twin is adopted and is transported to grow up in Italy. They are identical twins, so they have the same DNA. Assume both have a moderately high number of risk genes for RD. Based on what we know about culture, the twin being raised in Italy is at lower risk for RD than the co-twin growing up in the United States. The genes stay the same – the expression of those genes as the clinical phenotype RD differs based on the linguistic demands of the native language. A less demanding language structure makes genetic differences among individuals less relevant, without having any impact per se (structurally at least) on the risk genes.

MORE NUANCED MODELS OF GENE–ENVIRONMENT INTERPLAY FOR ADHD AND RD

Despite the high heritability estimates found for ADHD and RD, this line of thinking has encouraged recognition that environmental factors may play a role in their etiology. Much of this work has been conducted in designs that don't collect DNA or use genetically informative designs. For example, there are a host of pre- and perinatal factors, such as maternal smoking and drinking during pregnancy, that have been correlated with ADHD in a number of studies. Other types of psychosocial risks have been examined that may be influential during childhood, including low parental education and marital discord. While none of these factors have been demonstrated to "cause" ADHD, they represent empirically supported types of environmental risk that are associated with ADHD, in the same way that there is evidence for genes. It is noted here that while behavioral genetic studies have revealed genetic effects on these types of psychosocial risk factors, they are far from being "genetic" traits and are treated here as contextual influences that shape the expression of risk genes for ADHD. Put another way, if a child was placed in an environment in which parental education increased, or marital discord decreased, the assumption is that risk for ADHD would decrease, no matter what the genetic loading for it.

In addition to the liability model presented above – which postulates that environmental factors add up along with genetic propensity to shape risk for ADHD and RD – more recent thinking has embraced complementary models of gene–environment interplay. Most prominent have been suggestions that gene – environment interaction (GxE) models deserve consideration. Bear in mind that the GxE model differs from the liability model because the assumption is that the effects of genes are conditional on different levels of environmental risk – as opposed to simply adding up with environmental factors to create an overall vulnerability. If GxE is relevant, some kids will respond strongly to an environmental factor, whereas others will not, depending on the specific variants of a gene. In this model a given gene will not have an effect on risk unless it is paired with a specific type of environmental influence. It's the interplay between genes and environment that matter here, and that helps explain who is at higher or lower risk for a disorder.

A crucial consideration here is that the heritability estimate technically incorporates the effects of gene–environment interplay along with purely genetic effects. While this has been known for decades, the point had been obscured for many years, and is now being revisited given the growing interest in GxE. Evidence of substantial heritability may not only implicate genes – but also the environmental conditions under which they get expressed.

When we think about GxE, though, we typically focus on the studies which have examined specific genetic markers in conjunction with salient environmental risk factors. Most of the genes looked at to date are thought to be involved in the regulation of the neurotransmitter dopamine, as the stimulant medications most frequently used to treat ADHD involve dopaminergic functioning. Environmental factors have fallen into two broad classes – pre- and perinatal factors, and psychosocial influences.

Joel Nigg and colleagues (Nigg, Nikolas, & Burt, 2010) have provided a thoughtful overview of this approach and made an interesting observation – that the genes looked at most typically as risk factors for ADHD interact most strongly with psychosocial risk factors, and not so much with pre- and perinatal influences. In fact, the statistical effect of GxE when psychosocial factors were examined was twice that for models that focused on pre- and perinatal risk. In this review psychosocial factors included constructs like marital discord and adversity, whereas pre- and perinatal influences included known risks like maternal smoking and drinking. For example, Nikolas and colleagues (2012) have shown that parental conflict may be one key factor that characterizes the family climate and interacts with genetic propensity. At this stage, these kinds of results should be interpreted cautiously. They are dependent on the genes that are evaluated, and as we assume that there are many such genes, these initial studies have only focused on a small number of readily available markers that make biological sense. The findings are stronger for inattentive symptoms, raising the question of the importance of subtyping based on symptom profile. But what's especially important here is the notion that fundamental psychosocial risks – the kind that many children experience as they grow up – may be much more influential than we would have guessed if we treated the high heritability estimate of ADHD as indicating that this disorder is fundamentally due only to the effects of risk genes.

Jenni Rosenberg and colleagues (Rosenberg, Pennington, Willcutt, & Olson, 2012) offer an intriguing perspective that builds on this idea. Focusing on potential GxE models, they have suggested that ADHD and RD may reflect fundamentally different types of GxE. This insight has come from application of the twin study methodology, which can also be used to study GxE. Rosenberg and colleagues modeled statistically the effects of parental education – as a fundamental psychosocial factor – which has been shown to influence both ADHD and RD. They asked a fundamental question: does the heritability for ADHD, and RD, differ based on level of parental education. For ADHD, they found that the heritability estimate was substantially larger when parental education was lower. The interpretation was that this finding is best explained by a diathesis–stress GxE in which the effects of risk genes become influential only when the environmental risk is high. The idea here is that youth with an assumed high density of risk genes for ADHD may not express them behaviorally unless they are exposed to a high-risk environment. Put another way, the effects of the environment can override underlying genetic propensities – children with a high dosage of risk genes are not as likely to express high levels of ADHD when they are in a low-risk environment (here indicated as a higher level of parental education). Heritability in this model represents the level of reactivity to the risk environment. This perspective dovetails with the molecular genetic investigations of GxE, which suggested that psychosocial risk seems to differentially "activate" the effects of specific candidate genes that influence propensity for ADHD.

When the same methods and statistical models were applied to children with RD, there was again evidence for GxE – but in the opposite direction. Heritability was much higher in the low-risk or "protective" environment (high parental education) – and not so influential for kids in the low-risk environment. Rosenberg and colleagues (2012) referred to this as a bioecological GxE (in contrast to the more common diathesis–stress model). In the bioecological model low-risk environments obfuscate the role of genes because they have an especially powerful effect. It is more possible to see evidence of genetic risks for RD when the environment is protective, as it then becomes obvious that some kids still encounter difficulties with reading even though they have an environment that maximizes the potential for learning. It's noted that more than one study has found this pattern of results for RD.

There are two important implications from this line of work. First, heritability is a statistical indicator that could be used to provide insight into the types of environments in which genes may have more, or less, impact on shaping risk for disorders. It is clearly not a definitive measure that demonstrates that disorders such as ADHD and RD are inherently genetic in origin. Second, the distinction between the diathesis–stress and bioecological model is telling because it suggests that GxE may be nuanced and operate differently for different disorders. The contention here is that this is exactly the type of thinking – and information – that should be used to both support the potential importance of psychosocial intervention for highly heritable disorders like ADHD and RD, and suggest ways in which genetic information may in fact help us think about how different types of interventions may be tailored to genetic risk.

THE PROMISE OF PSYCHOSOCIAL INTERVENTIONS

The conceptual and empirical work described above provides a very strong platform for psychosocial interventions for RD and ADHD. Such interventions certainly exist and as we will see have been shown to have utility. The recommendation here is that these interventions be thought of as primary, and as the most likely route to making meaningful changes in the life of a child with RD, or with ADHD. They shouldn't be seen as being lesser attempts at intervention until we find the magic bullets from genetic research that will be translated into tailored intervention. It's hard to imagine what those magic bullets will be given the complexity of the number of genes involved and the potential interplay with the environment. Rather psychosocial interventions that acknowledge the strong role that context and the psychosocial environment may play in conjunction with genetic risk may eventually offer more targeted intervention opportunities than those driven simply by genomic profiles.

Let's take an example that illustrates the current bias towards biology for highly heritable disorders like ADHD and the need for more appreciation of the role of the psychosocial environment for both shaping, and changing, the developmental course of at risk youth. There is much debate about the utility of diagnosing ADHD in preschool children (as young as 4 years of age). The argument for doing this stems from the idea that ADHD is often persistent, and without treatment, can lead to a cascade of effects that get worse with each developmental stage. It's also suggested that kids with high levels of ADHD can be observed reliably in the preschool years, and their impairment – especially in terms of peer interactions and to a lesser extent behavior in the classroom – and as such should be treated immediately.

When we think realistically about the type of treatment preschoolers with ADHD will receive, the first one on the list is pharmacology. Stimulants are a staple of the treatment regimen and some have been approved for use in children as young as 3 years of age. There are many studies that have shown improvement in overall functioning (both reductions in ADHD symptoms and gains in academic and social outcomes) attributable to drug intervention. Since ADHD is thought of as a biological disorder – and one that is probably genetic in origin – it would seem logical that the primary point to offering a diagnosis in the preschool years is to support initiation of pharmacology as the treatment of choice.

Initial investigations evaluating the efficacy of drug treatments on toddlers with ADHD have yielded a complex picture

(Ghuman & Ghuman, 2013). While there is some evidence of improvement, a number of adverse effects have been reported. Furthermore, it is noted that there is limited information on the effects of the common forms of psychopharmacology on the developing brain of the toddler. Does that mean we need to devise different drug treatments that are tailored to preschoolers? Use genetic methods to lead this charge? Or question the idea that we are prescribing drugs that are not even tailored to the disorder at ages for which little data exist on long-term effects?

This situation highlights the reality of where we are at a decade after completion of the HGP. We simply do not have genes in hand that can be used to diagnose ADHD or even predict elevated risk. We are questioning if we will ever be able to reduce the anticipated number of genes that would be involved into a deliverable indicator that would serve these purposes. As such, we are pretty far away from devising one of the expected outcomes of the HGP – the development of targeted interventions that are tailored to gene functions and products.

As it's becoming evident that the assumed strong effect of genes on ADHD can be shaped by psychosocial factors, it's time to take much more seriously the idea that psychosocial interventions should be invested in heavily at a national level (both conceptually and financially) – and with the same amount of research effort devoted to the genetics of ADHD. There are in fact a number of psychosocial strategies that have been used and evaluated to date. Some interventions are geared more toward improving school behavior and are directed toward correcting deficits in performance (e.g., how to apply a skill like sitting still and listening with more consistency) and/or teaching new skills (like learning to follow directions). Others focus on improving the parent–child relationship and encouraging parenting strategies that help shape regulated and directed behavior. These can include constructs like learning how to set up an appropriate and consistently administered reward system, and using strategies for effective communication. These are basic parenting skills that can be challenging to implement when a child has high levels of symptoms of ADHD.

The thinking is that these types of psychosocial interventions can be quite effective (see, for example, Watson, Richels, Michalek, & Raymer, 2012). Bear in mind that the parenting strategies, in particular, dovetail nicely with the primary findings from the first generation of GxE studies of ADHD, which strongly implicated the role of family climate and parenting behaviors as a context in which genes are expressed. This is vastly different than "blaming" bad parenting as cause of ADHD. Rather it's a realistic perspective that suggests parenting can make a difference – for good or for bad – and as such, changing parenting should be influential. Clinical experience would certainly back up this claim. But while psychosocial interventions for ADHD have been examined empirically, the reality is that there is a paucity of data on them as compared to the very large literature on the behavioral and molecular genetics of ADHD. Recent reviews of psychosocial interventions suggest that many more studies need to be conducted to understand more about why and how they work – and how they can be sharpened. The contention here is that this is unlikely to be a major emphasis of research funding because of the assumption that ADHD is a genetic disorder.

An alternate viewpoint is that we can support further genetic research on ADHD – it's certainly important – but within the context of evaluating psychosocial interventions that have the promise of changing children's behavior immediately, not a decade (or two, or three, or four) from now. The diathesis–stress model is certainly a good platform for understanding the importance of psychosocial processes in the etiology of ADHD and the potential utility of reducing risk for ADHD by environmental means. The implication of the diathesis–stress model is that reducing psychosocial risk will help prevent some kids who are at presumed genetic risk for ADHD from manifesting high levels of symptomatology. While it's not possible to make an empirical guess at the actual reduction of rates of diagnosed ADHD that would result from application of promising psychosocial methods – particularly those that emphasize the teaching of parenting skills that may be especially effective with kids who have symptoms – it can be stated with certainty that the success will be much greater than what we have now as tailored biological treatments. We have none of those. While there are newer drugs on the market for ADHD, the reality is that the standard treatment of choice is an approach that far outdates the completion of the HGP.

If we take an optimistic perspective on molecular genetic research on ADHD and assume more and more risk genes will be identified and replicated, the point here is to start putting them into the mix when looking at the efficacy of psychosocial interventions. That's where the traction may lie in terms of getting a better handle on why these interventions may work for some youth and not others. And it's at least a platform for developing newer frameworks that prioritize intervention studies as a way of actually doing something with the accumulating genetic database. Doesn't it make more sense to implement – on a large scale – these kinds of trials rather than spending time and money evaluating drug treatments of preschoolers? And while slowly chipping away at candidate genes and conducting expensive genome-wide association studies is important, how much of this information is going to trickle down to actually improving the lives of children who have ADHD right now?

The same case can be made for RD. There are a number of remedial programs that are offered for children with RD that are geared to the type of neurocognitive deficits observed (see Snowling & Hulme, 2012). For example, many schools offer comprehensive remedial programs such as Ortin Gillington, which focuses on the processing difficulties and offers a number of methods to improve reading ability over time. Some youth can make substantial improvements in developmental level over time – and some can at least learn strategies for compensating for difficulties in multiple components of reading. To date, these types of interventions have been far removed from the genetic laboratory – and the argument here is that it would be profitable to think about changing that.

Think back to the bioecological model invoked earlier as a framework for understanding how parental education interacts with genetic risk for RD. One principle was that genetic influences on RD are not as detectable when parental education was low. While low parental education does not necessarily imply an impoverished cognitive upbringing, it is the case that many children in the United States do not experience the appropriate environmental stimulation to develop essential pre-literacy skills. In many cases this could be rectified by environmental intervention especially in the preschool years. There are indeed a number of initiatives that take on this task and attempt to promote school readiness. For example, the Thrive in Five partnership in Boston links efforts between the city and the United Way to provide support and training to families so that they can offer toddlers the kind of early learning environments they need to promote school readiness – including key pre-literacy skills. While the success of programs like Thrive in Five will be evaluated empirically, again it is not an overstatement to suggest that they carry much more promise for changing children's lives today than any immediate deliverable from genetics.

This is not to say that genetics doesn't play a role, and potentially an important one. Rather the bioecological model suggests that the role of genes may be more clearly appreciated when environmental risk is low. This is not a new principle in genetics – the general idea has been around for a long time – but it's now one that can be acted upon given the advances in molecular genetics. Like any genetic strategy, it would require dedicated effort to secure the requisite sample sizes. But since we do that anyway, why not apply the genetic methodology within a broader initiative to offer large-scale environmental intervention for RD? On the one hand, environmental initiatives would, based on the bioecological model, have impact on a number of children who are at environmental risk because the environment – and not DNA – is having a disproportionate effect on propensity for RD. That said, evaluating in detail children who have RD despite intensive psychosocial intervention may provide insight into the more "pure" genetic form or get us somewhat closer to the "perfect phenotype" for genetic analysis. The environment would have both the power to alter risk and illuminate the effects of genes. But this will not happen unless we aggressively treat environmental interventions for RD as big science and merge it with the very large science of genetics.

CONCLUDING REMARKS

This chapter provided an integrated look at both ADHD and RD. Examining these disorders together reflects a bias towards convergence between etiological models for disorders rather than a purely phenotypic approach, which would examine each disorder separately. ADHD and RD share much in common in terms of an overarching etiological model. They are both highly heritable and as such have been interpreted as genetic disorders. But, as shown here, "heritable" does not necessarily imply no role for the environment, even when the estimates are extremely high – heritability is defined in part by context and technically may embed gene–environment interplay. We considered a number of models that take on potential ways in which genes and environment may intersect for each disorder and found evidence supporting the role of the psychosocial environment for both ADHD and RD. Recent suggestions highlight different forms of GxE for each disorder – both of which emphasize how environment risks can have main effects that override genetic influences and can serve as the context that elicits the impact of genes. Various psychosocial interventions were introduced as examples of approaches that could be merged synergistically with genetic methodologies, allowing both a platform for studying gene–environment interplay and the delivery of potentially effective approaches that could have large positive impacts on the developmental trajectories of a number of young children.

Seasoned clinicians will often talk about the importance of psychosocial intervention for ADHD and RD and how all best efforts should be made to change the psychosocial environment for a child who is suspected of having ADHD. Only after these best efforts are applied does it make sense to then consider the utility of pharmacology. We know of course that youth can benefit from pharmacology, and some benefit greatly. But it is not a panacea, and it is unlikely to be tailored substantially in the coming years by data from the genetic laboratory. Our best hope for using the advances on the genetics of ADHD and RD that will be coming our way will be to cross it with intensive efforts to test out empirically environmental interventions. We might then someday find much more tailored ways of shaping the environment to improve the lives of youth with ADHD and RD and perhaps understand better ways of circumventing high levels of genetic liability to these disorders.

REFERENCES

Ghuman, J. K., & Ghuman, H. S. (2013). Pharmacologic intervention for attention-deficit hyperactivity disorder in preschoolers: Is it justified? *Paediatric Drugs*, *15*, 1–8.

Nigg, J., Nikolas, M., & Burt, S. A. (2010). Measured gene by environment interaction in relation to attention-deficit/hyperactivity disorder (ADHD). *Journal of the American Academy of Child and Adolescent Psychiatry*, *49*, 863–873.

Nikolas, M., Klump, K. L., & Burt, S. A. (2012). Youth appraisals of inter-parental conflict and genetic and environmental contributions to attention-deficit hyperactivity disorder: Examination of GxE effects in a twin sample. *Journal of Abnormal Child Psychology*, *40*, 543–554.

Rosenberg, J., Pennington, B. F., Willcutt, E. G., & Olson, R. K. (2012). Gene by environment interactions influencing reading disability (RD) and the inattentive symptom dimension of attention deficit/hyperactivity disorder (ADHD). *Journal of Child Psychology and Psychiatry*, *53*, 243–251.

Skiba, T., Landi, N., Wagner, R., & Grigorenko, E. L. (2011). In search of the perfect phenotype: An analysis of linkage and association studies of reading and reading-related processes. *Behavior Genetics*, *41*, 6–30.

Snowling, M. J., & Hulme, C. (2012). Interventions for children's language and literacy difficulties. *International Journal of Language and Communication Disorders*, *47*, 27–34.

Thapar, A., Cooper, M., Eyre, O., & Langley, K. (2013). What have we learned about the causes of ADHD? *Journal of Child Psychology and Psychiatry*, *54*, 3–16.

Watson, S. M., Richels, C., Michalek, A. P., & Raymer, A. (2012). Psychosocial treatments for ADHD: A systematic appraisal of the evidence. *Journal of Attention Disorders*, http://jad.sagepub.com/content/early/2012/05/29/1087054712447857.abstract

CHAPTER

4

Conduct Problems and Substance Use: The Underappreciated Role of Shared Environmental Influences

We have learned a lot about conduct problems (CP) over the past few decades. We know that onset during childhood is predictive of a troubling developmental future, including the likelihood of escalating behavioral issues, difficulties in school, association with delinquent peers, and potential arrests. Note here the use of the broader construct of CP to cover youth who either meet diagnostic criteria for conduct disorder (CD) or have been shown to have high levels of delinquent behaviors across developmental stages. While CD is the clinical diagnosis of choice, the reality is that most of the informative longitudinal studies have used continuous measures and quantitative approaches to identify kids with profiles of persistent CP and as such we will be extracting heavily from this work.

Early onset of CP is also a robust risk factor for early-onset substance use (SU), which portends even more dire outcomes. Initiation of SU in early adolescence – whether it be smoking, drinking, marijuana use, or use of other substances – has potentially severe effects on the emerging development of the brain during adolescence, often involves relationship difficulties (peer and romantic) and negative social influences, and may prime an individual for rapid acceleration to problematic levels of use along with polysubstance use. It also predicts a number of serious difficulties in early adulthood, including risk for substance abuse and dependence, health problems, and incarceration.

You can observe of all these unfortunate possibilities if you spend time in a juvenile court. The youth that come through that system often show clearly persistent delinquent behaviors and sometimes especially aggressive ones. Indeed, many of them have a developmental history of CP and clear evidence of escalating problem behaviors. The vast majority of them will have initiated substance use by their early teens and may already show signs of abuse. As a general rule, the home life is far from optimal – and if you could evaluate the quality of parenting, you will find in many cases the need for more effective child-rearing methods.

If you probed further into the family dynamics, you would find that most of the youth have a sibling – which is not surprising since nearly 85% of youth have at least one sibling. What might be surprising is that most of the siblings will show evidence of the same developmental trajectory. Siblings are typically highly correlated for conduct problems, both delinquent and aggressive in nature. Siblings are also very similar with respect to early initiation of SU. Older siblings of the youth in a juvenile detention facility would undoubtedly show a history of extremely high rates of CP and SU (including early-onset use prior to the legal age). In a study that is currently ongoing, my collaborators and I have observed this as we recruited adolescents with alcohol-related difficulties as well as their siblings – over 95% of the older siblings of these teens were using substances prior to the legal age (and most of them were using more than one substance). Sibling similarity for CP and SU in adolescence has been replicated across many samples (both in the United States and around the world) over the past few decades. In many studies, having an older sibling who smokes or drinks is a powerful predictor of SU and typically more influential than parental SU. The magnitude of effect of having an older sibling who uses substances is often greater than many other risk factors, and continues to emerge in published papers as a key social predictor of early-onset SU (only exceeded in predictive value by having a best friend who uses substances).

Such strong evidence of sibling similarity for CP and SU does not imply evidence for genes or environment, as familial correlations and associations can be due to either or a combination of both. As discussed in prior chapters, the fundamental statistical model used in behavioral genetics has always provided estimates of environmental influence along with the effects of genes. Here again the two classes of environmental factors considered in behavioral genetic models are important to consider – those that operate to make siblings similar on a trait (shared environment) and those that make them different (nonshared environment). And we saw surprising evidence for a primary role for shared environmental influences on autism spectrum disorder (ASD), which has, to a degree, influenced thinking about the importance of the environment for what has been thought of (for a long time now) as a genetic disorder.

That has come about from the results of one twin study of ASD. Consider, then, the potential implications about the role of shared environment that would come from robust and replicable evidence drawn from a number of studies executed over the last decade, using different genetically informative designs and a variety of measures. Such is the case for both CP and SU. As we will see, the etiological models for both constructs are essentially the same – due in no small part to the idea that they probably have common social roots (which will be discussed). But while this body of work has been widely published in top-flight journals – and in fact accepted by most experts in behavioral genetics – it has certainly not had the broader clout of genetic work in the post–HGP era. It's not the type of work that generates press releases and national discussion about the importance of social environments in the lives of children. You don't see large-scale initiatives by funding institutes that are driven by these data and launched to target potentially changeable features of the environment that are being shown to put many youth at risk for a predictable trajectory of maladaptive development and compromised health. The argument here is that the strong implications of this body of work need to put in a spotlight, and the rest of this chapter will lay out the reasons why, along with the very real implications for the urgency of ramping up our efforts to support psychosocial interventions.

GENETIC MODELS OF CP AND SU

There have been many studies examining genetic and environmental influences on CP. They have consistently supported the idea that genes play a role. The heritability estimates have been lower than what we have seen for other disorders like ASD, attention–deficit/hyperactivity disorder (ADHD), and reading disorder (RD), but nonetheless significant. Fair to say that, across studies, they represent statistically "moderate" effects of genes. All the evidence to date is consistent with the idea we have seen for other forms of psychopathology in youth – it is most likely that there are a number of genes that each have a small effect on risk for CP. There is, without question, no evidence of major gene effects – and no universally accepted candidate genes that are uniquely predictive of CP.

The idea that genes play some role is undoubtedly important. Some scholars like Terrie Moffitt (see Moffitt, 1993) have suggested – for some time now – that biological factors may play a particularly strong role for some kids who have early onset of CP, which represents the start of a persistent pattern of maladaptive behavior across the lifespan. Recent work implies that CP is especially onerous if a child has high levels of callous-emotional traits – which may have an even stronger genetic basis. And if we orient our perspective toward adulthood, constructs like antisocial personality disorder (ASP) are typically shown to be highly heritable. So it's clear that there is some influence of genes, even though the number of genes and the biological pathways of influence are yet to be specified.

The same can be said about SU. There is certainly evidence for genetic influence on SU in adolescence – with heritability estimates being in the more moderate range. Since we are talking about early initiation and use of substances, we would be thinking about genetically influenced traits that might affect the likelihood of gravitating toward social situations and contexts that promote and encourage risk-taking behavior. Matt McGue and colleagues have examined a construct of behaviors called "behavioral disinhibition" that are associated with SU in adolescence and show evidence of significant heritability and potentially a candidate phenotype for genetic analysis (see McGue et al., 2013). These can be thought of as a mix of personality traits – like risk taking and impulsivity – that convey a nonspecific risk for SU and in fact overlap with traits associated with CP. A different tradition of work has looked for more specific indicators of genetic risk for reactivity to substances, like initial reactions to a first cigarette. While these approaches are conceptually of interest, they have not yet provided strong replicable evidence of genetic influence in genetically informative designs. Like CP, when adult constructs are examined – like substance abuse and dependence – we tend to see stronger implication for genetic effects as heritability estimates increase.

So there are strong parallels to the genetic models of CP and SU. There is evidence supporting a role for genes that makes conceptual sense. We have speculation – but less firm data – that there may be underlying subtypes or specific behavioral indicators (e.g., childhood-onset CP, callous-unemotional traits, reactions to first cigarette) that may reflect stronger genetic signals. It seems clear that the relative impact of genes becomes stronger in adulthood as the behaviors become more problematic and impairing. There is nothing in the literature to suggest that major genes (genes with a disproportionate impact on the developmental course of youth) have been, or will be, found for CP and SU – rather the basic additive model of genetic effects (many genes of small effect size that combine to increase the likelihood of CP and SU) best describes the findings to date from genetically informative studies. Given that there is evidence for only moderate genetic effects, we also know (by default) that the environment must matter in the statistical models. And as we will now see, there is a very consistent picture that has emerged in the published literature.

THE IMPACT OF SHARED ENVIRONMENTAL INFLUENCES

Most of the behavioral genetic literature over the past few decades has emphasized two explanatory processes – genetics and nonshared environment. A simple way to think about it is that for most traits studied, similarity between family members has been best "explained" by genetics (via the heritability estimate), with familial dissimilarity being due to nonshared environmental factors (environmental influences that are unique to an individual and not common to family members). This general model has been efficient for a number of traits, particularly those in the cognitive and personality domains. We saw how this type of summary model also applied to ADHD and RD – and until very recently to ASD. While some evidence for shared environment creeps up now and then in general, it has been dismissed in the vast majority of the most parsimonious statistical models.

This behavioral genetic rule of thumb has not, however, applied so well to CP and SU – and this has been in the air for a number of decades. For example, the late David Rowe applied the phrase "partners in crime" in the 1980s to describe the pattern of results he observed when he examined twin similarity for delinquent behavior – a pattern in which twins were very highly correlated whether they were identical or fraternal twins and showed evidence of committing delinquent acts together (see Rowe, 1983). Two ideas were important here. First, twins were very similar to each other, suggesting that CP "runs" in families. But in contrast to the typical behavioral genetic model, the primary source for their similarity was environmental, not genetic – and hence, the putative role of shared environment was emphasized. Rowe went one step further though – his infusion of the "partners in crime" concept reflected his belief that siblings were not just similar, but in fact directly involved in behaviorally encouraging and shaping each other's CP. He also expanded this idea (in the early 1990s) to include SU in early adolescence – which he captured via the phrase "sibling effects" (see Rowe & Gulley, 1992).

This pioneering work has stood the test of time and continues to be replicated and expanded in important ways, as will be discussed below. But before highlighting current informative studies, it's worth considering one key methodological point that makes the conclusions drawn to date even more powerful – a number of genetically informative designs have all shown evidence for strong shared environmental effects. In prior chapters, we focused on the classic twin method that compares identical and fraternal twins. While informative, this design certainly has limitations, as does any natural experiment. Historically the strongest concern has been centered on the "equal environments assumption" – the assumption in the twin modeling that MZ and DZ twins have equal environments. Put another way, the general biometrical model assumes that there are no unique environmental correlates of having an identical twin versus having a fraternal twin. Of course, this assumption can be tested empirically and, to varying degrees, has been shown to be a modest limitation of the twin method.

Beyond the equal environments assumption, a more general issue is the extent to which data from twin studies generalize to non-twin populations. Whether identical or fraternal, twins are the same age – and it is not clear how much that simple fact may influence the patterning we see in the data. That's when alternative genetically informative designs can provide especially important insights. We can gauge empirically how well the twin data generalize to other types of genetic relationships among siblings.

We will consider two such designs that have been especially important in studying CP and SU. One approach involves expansions of the twin design to incorporate non-twin biological siblings, as well as half-siblings and biologically unrelated siblings. From the genetic perspective, we have more information on genetic relatedness to model. We know that in the twin design MZ twins are assumed to share 100% of their genes, whereas DZ twins are assumed to share, on average, 50% of their genes. As DZ twins are just biological siblings who are born at the same time, they provide an interesting contrast to biological siblings, who have the same genetic gradient but differ in terms of age gap. Half-siblings share, on average, 25% of their genes. And unrelated siblings – in these designs biologically unrelated children who are being raised together (in some cases because of remarriage rather than adoption) – share, on average, 0% of these genes. Without going into all the details, it should be appreciated that there is much room here for expanding the basic twin design in this way to incorporate additional levels of genetic relatedness and also include siblings who would not have "twin effects."

Such expansions of the twin study – particularly inclusion of nonbiological siblings who are reared together – are complemented by the sibling adoption method. Adoption studies have a long history of informing our understanding of genetics and environment, as they clearly separate out the effects of genetics from those of the rearing environment. Here the most relevant design that has been used of late is to focus on nonbiological siblings who are adopted into a family and raised together. As was the case with the variants of the twin design, the similarity of adoptive siblings can be compared to the similarity of biological siblings (being raised together) to form another lens to examine how genes and environment contribute to behavioral development.

Given this perspective, there is clear-cut convergence across studies that support an unusual finding for genetically informative studies – particularly strong evidence for shared environmental effects. Simply put, environmental influences promote similarity among family members for CP and SU, especially when we focus on siblings. Alexandra Burt and colleagues have published a number of papers (see, for example, Burt,

McGue, & Iacono, 2010; Burt, Klahr, Rueter, McGue, & Iacono, 2011) that have provided compelling evidence that shared environmental influences are robust and replicable for CP in childhood and adolescence. Much of this work has been conducted within the SIBS (Sibling Interaction Behavior Study) project housed at the University of Minnesota, which studies adoptive and biological siblings and their parents. But as mentioned above, the evidence for shared environmental effects is especially influential because it cuts across designs.

This point is well illustrated by a recent paper that utilized data from three samples – two twin projects (the Oregon Twin Project or OTP, and the Michigan State University Twin Registry or MSUTR) and a combined twin-sibling design (the Nonshared Environment in Adolescent Development or NEAD) – to model estimates of genetic and environmental influences on externalizing behavior (a construct similar to CP) in middle childhood and adolescence (see Marceau et al., 2012). Across all three studies, data were available on identical twins, fraternal twins, biological siblings, half-siblings, and unrelated siblings. The evidence for shared environment was clear with the magnitude described as moderate to large across all three samples (ranging from 38% to 77%) and evident in both middle childhood and adolescence. The magnitude of genetic influence was less evident (significant only in adolescence) and lesser than what was found for shared environment. To be clear, the point here is not that the genes don't matter (they do), but rather that the shared environment is (contrary to conventional wisdom) potent and should be considered as seriously as genes in etiological models of CP.

The same conclusion is drawn when we consider adolescent substance use, as recent reviews have shown this to be the case for tobacco use, alcohol use, and marijuana use. Shared environmental effects are found to be robust whether the focus is on initiation (e.g., classifying subjects into having tried a substance versus not having tried a substance) or level of use in adolescence (e.g., quantifying usage such as the number of days out of the past month that a given substance was used). This finding has held up across country of origin as well as study design (so that it is not just found, for example, in the classic twin method). The consistency of the findings across methods and samples may thus speak to a particularly strong current of environmental influence on initial use of substances in adolescence.

To illustrate the basis for this claim, consider the patterns we've observed when analyzing data from the genetically informative component of the National Longitudinal Study of Adolescent Health (or Add Health). Like the NEAD discussed above, the Add Health project sampled a full range of genetic relatedness in sibling pairs by including identical twins, fraternal twins, full biological siblings, half-siblings, and unrelated siblings. Our published papers using data from Add Health have shown the strong evidence for shared environmental influences on both smoking and drinking in adolescence – something that can be seen quite readily in the basic descriptive data.

If we ignored (for the moment) genetic relatedness, siblings who are reared together (typically defined in studies as living together for a minimum number of years) are quite similar in their usage in adolescence: they are more likely to have either initiated or not initiated use, and if they have initiated use, they use at similar levels. When we then factor in genetic relatedness, we see that a good deal of sibling similarity is explained by environmental rather than genetic factors – there are nongenetic influences that account for their similar tendency to use or not use. For example, biologically unrelated siblings are quite similar in their use of substances (even though they do not share genes in the genetic epidemiological sense), and their level of similarity is not far off from biological siblings (who share on average half of their genes) and in fact monozygotic twins (who share all of their genes). The point here is that when a genetically informative design is used to "control" for genetic factors, there is strong evidence that environmental factors exert a powerful influence on adolescent substance use – and these influences promote similarity in siblings, suggesting some form of common or shared environmental effect (as is the case with CP as well).

GETTING MOLECULAR ABOUT THE ENVIRONMENT

If we go back decades in behavioral genetic research, we can see that the continual replication of evidence of heritability for a number of disorders and traits provided a firm foundation for serious forays into studying the genetics of complex phenotypes. There was a convergence between the mounting support of genetic models that suggested the utility of searching for a number of risk genes that each might play some role in etiology and methods that made this search possible (the platform for association and candidate gene studies). For nearly every trait and disorder in question, we had nothing more than significant heritability estimates that replicated across samples (typically drawn from twin studies).

Such a strategy was certainly productive in terms of generating a formidable amount of genetic research aimed at elusive genes of small effect – undoubtedly the best direction given all the available evidence. The point here is that the same philosophy should hold when we see these same genetically informative designs yield consistent evidence of shared environmental influences for specific traits and disorders such as CP and SU. Yet we do not see nearly the same enterprise – or enthusiasm – devoted to digging deeper to identify specific sources of shared environmental influences on CP and SU – even though our biometrical models point clearly in that direction. It's not so much that the evidence for the importance of shared environmental influences is disputed. Many behavioral genetic papers – written by leaders in the field – certainly acknowledge how the social environment is a prime shaper of the earliest experiences with substances. We are seeing more thrust in the literature recognizing the impact of shared environmental influences on CP. It's simply that these findings don't translate into the same type of dedicated and forceful programs of research funding and initiatives that we see for genetics.

There are in fact many good examples of how we can be more "molecular" in identifying the sources of shared environmental influences on CP and SU. Just as we speculate that there can be a large number of genes of small effect for any behavior phenotype, there may be multiple streams of environmental influence that affect the likelihood of CP and SU in childhood and adolescence. What's essential here is that genetically informative designs are used to isolate not just putative environmental influences but in fact specific mediators of part of the overall shared environmental effect. Simply studying "environmental" factors without a genetically informative component will not push this work forward.

Consider more studies conducted by Burt and colleagues (2009, 2010, 2011). In the three sample studies described above (combining data from the OTP, the MSUTR, and the NEAD), the strongest evidence for shared environmental influences on externalizing behavior was gathered when observational measures were used. As discussed by the study authors, there are many advantages to using observational methods, with a primary one being that rater bias – a typical concern when collecting perceptions of parents and teachers – is minimized. The argument can also be made that observational data provide a fundamental insight into relationship dynamics and family process that go beyond assessing perceptions of family members.

With these thoughts in mind, Burt's work with collaborators on the SIBS project provides an excellent illustration of how we can begin to discern specific social processes that contribute to the shared environmental effect on externalizing behavior including CP (see Klahr, McGue, Iacono, & Burt, 2011). Parent–child conflict is a well replicated predictor of CP and hence a good candidate "SE" (shared environment) factor. In this SIBS study, both observational and informant measures of parent–child conflict and CP were utilized. Phenotypically, parent–child conflict was highly associated with levels of CP in the adolescents. The sibling adoption design, however, permitted further insight into the potential environmental pathways underlying this association. First, consider the insight that can be gained by studying parent–child conflict and CP in adoptive families. Here there is no genetic pathway that would link parent–child conflict and CP (unless there is a substantial influence of selective placement – in which parents and offspring are "matched" during the adoptive process based on certain characteristics – which does not appear to be a factor). Any association would be inferred to reflect an environmental process – and this is exactly what is seen in the data that supports a strong link between parent–child conflict and CP. Furthermore, the strength of this association is not very different in the biological families, suggesting that genetic relatedness does not make a substantial additional impact on familial transmission of risk. More formal analyses of the data showed that, in the parlance of behavior genetics, the shared environmental effect was in fact significantly mediated by parent–child conflict – and this finding generalized to both observational and informant data.

In another paper these authors took these findings one step further. They showed that parent–child conflict was predictive of CP over a 4-year timespan – whereas CP did not predict later parent–child conflict. The implication here is that there is a directional effect whereby parent–child conflict directly increases the level of CP over time. Again, by demonstrating this association – now expanded longitudinally – in adoptive families, we eliminate the possibility of genetic factors "explaining" this linkage. The point here is not to dismiss the idea that genes may play some role too. Rather, it's to emphasize that shared environment is, in the case of CP, a very strong influence over time, a directional predictor, and a potentially modifiable risk factor in a child's life, with parent–child conflict serving as one concrete behavioral target for intervention. And, simply put, it is a primary pathway by which siblings growing up in the same family are similar in terms of their trajectory for CP.

Another example comes from research on direct sibling effects on adolescent substance use. From the perspective of intervention, social dynamics between siblings and mutual friendships have stood out as explanatory factors within the genetic epidemiological models, particularly for tobacco use and alcohol use. Assessing the amount of time that siblings spend together, and whether or not they have mutual friends, explains a good portion of the shared environmental effect on adolescent substance use (as we have shown in modeling data from the Add Health project). These findings have been interpreted as a form of social contagion in our own studies, as it involves shared environmental mechanisms and implies direct interaction between siblings as a causative risk factor (see Rende, Slomkowski, Lloyd-Richardson, & Niaura, 2005; Slomkowski, Rende, Novak, Lloyd-Richardson, & Niaura, 2005). For example, if an older sibling has been introduced to substances by a friend, and if a younger sibling is close in age and spends time with the older sibling and the friend, the younger sibling may initiate use earlier than would be expected. A corollary to that scenario is that lack of appropriate parental monitoring and limit sets up a particularly conducive family environment for social contagion, both in terms of siblings within the family being more likely to be exposed to substance use by peers and friends and also directly affecting each other's likelihood of use. Interestingly, analyses that we are currently conducting suggest that this sibling contagion process is not limited to early adolescence – we are seeing evidence of this same dynamic contributing to levels of cigarette and alcohol use in the late teen years and in the early twenties.

A DEVELOPMENTAL GENE–ENVIRONMENT MODEL

How does this "contagion" model of initiation of substance use in adolescence connect with risk for progression to higher levels of use, including abuse and dependence? In genetically informative studies – particularly prospective longitudinal projects – the genetic and environmental influences underlying progression have been examined. Here a very different story has emerged: the role of shared environmental factors appears to be of negligible importance in that it does not explain sibling similarity for higher levels of tobacco, alcohol, or marijuana use. What *does* explain sibling similarity for progression of substance use is genetic influence. Going back to our prior example, biologically unrelated siblings who were shown to be highly similar in their tendency to initiate use of substances will not be very similar in their likelihood to go on to higher levels of use, including abuse and dependence. In contrast, monozygotic twins who were shown to be highly similar in terms of initiation will also show a high degree of similarity for progression to regular use in adulthood as well as abuse and dependence. The inference is that progression is due to common genetic factors, which the unrelated siblings do not share. It is important to emphasize that the strong evidence suggesting genetic influence on progression from initiation to varying levels of misuse and abuse cuts across the primary substances studied (tobacco, alcohol, and marijuana).

Indeed, the findings from most behavioral genetic studies – which emphasize shared environmental influences on initiation and early use, and genetic influences on progression – sits well with the arguments made previously in support of intervention aimed at adolescent substance use by bringing into play a unifying developmental model. This "two-stage" model suggests different classes of influence that may dominate at different points in the trajectory. It supports strongly the idea that psychosocial factors may be particularly important in terms of shaping risk for early use of substances – but these same factors are not so relevant when we consider why some adolescents progress to problematic use while others do not. So we have here a first piece of a developmental gene–environment model – an emphasis on the psychosocial climate of peer and family influences and a number of interconnected risk factors that could serve as rational and empirically supported targets for psychosocial intervention. What is noteworthy here is the idea that *genetically informative studies* have yielded a consensus that implicates *environmental* risk processes anchored at a specific developmental stage and thus supports directly the idea that *psychosocial intervention* may be particularly effective in reducing substance use in early adolescence.

What about the role of genes? Well, let's consider again the literature that suggests initial levels of exposure to substances – which, as we have seen, is strongly influenced by psychosocial factors – leads only some adolescents to problematic use, in part via putative individual differences in biological risk and also shaping of brain responses to substances. A logical argument is that these individual differences are highly related to genetic differences, and that the mode of action for risk genes is to become activated and increase an individual's susceptibility to eventual abuse and addiction. There is an emerging, and rapidly expanding and changing, empirical base to support the typically small effect of a number of candidate genes, particularly those implicated in either metabolism of addictive chemicals or the activity of brain reward areas. Although most of the evidence has come from studies of adults, there have been some reports that focus on adolescence.

So, for example, there are specific genes – which are thought to play a role in the metabolism of nicotine – that have been associated with risk for nicotine dependence. Other studies have provided evidence that some genes may be linked with those initial reactions to smoking (e.g., relaxation versus nausea). A similar perspective exists for alcohol use: there are studies that support the role of a number of genes that seem to increase likelihood of developing alcohol abuse and dependence, and there are also genes that make it highly unlikely that some individuals will use alcohol because they moderate strong negative reactions to alcohol exposure (e.g., vomiting). Overall, the idea is that many of the genes that may eventually be implicated in various forms of substance abuse and dependence will essentially relate to how individuals *react* to exposure to the substance.

The point is that psychosocial interventions would likely not *directly* affect these biological predispositions to escalating use and abuse of substances. Rather, psychosocial interventions may be conceptualized as having the potential for *indirect* effects on the genetic pathways by blocking continual use of substances that are believed to "turn on" these genes that react to the active addictive chemicals in tobacco, alcohol, and marijuana. Let's refer back to the idea that is currently in the air – that exposure to substances adversely affects the developing adolescent brain. Putting our pieces together, the opportunity (and challenge) for researchers is to see if some adolescents are particularly susceptible to this reactivity because of the effects of specific genes (which either predispose toward or protect against addiction). Specifically, recent studies are just beginning to suggest that entire systems of genes may be "turned on" when exposed to a substance. For example, one study identified nearly one hundred genes that become activated when a person smokes a cigarette. It is this cascading effect of substance exposure, crossed with activation of risk genes, that may portend eventual abuse and dependence by adversely priming the adolescent brain.

At this point, we have the basis for a framework for one model of psychosocial intervention: *to prevent eventual gene expression using environmental intervention*. What is especially notable about the prior and ongoing genetically informative work is that essential roles of environmental and genetic risk factors are being articulated, along with the way in which they intersect in developmental time. This is much more helpful than blanket statements that would suggest in a generic way that environment and genes come together to create risk for substance use and abuse. In particular, we have almost a mandate from this body of work to consider the psychosocial environment of initiation and early usage of substances in adolescence as a template for targeted interventions that could focus on social processes (e.g., parenting, sibling, and peer influences). Clinicians, in turn, are given a platform to consider how their interventions may in turn be conceptualized as a possible blockade for genetically moderated progression of use through adolescence and beyond. Of course, at this point this is simply a model – an attractive heuristic that refines the role of the clinician in the postgenomic era of research on substance use. The next section of this chapter will introduce one psychosocial intervention, and the last section will cover recent studies that point the way toward direct integration of family-based interventions with genetic methods.

FAMILY-BASED INTERVENTIONS AND GENETIC EPIDEMIOLOGY

There are a number of psychosocial interventions that have been applied to attempt to reduce levels of substance use in adolescence. They can be tailored to specific substances or be more generic with respect to use of any substances. They can focus on a number of domains – including family, school, and community-level factors – along with intersections of these areas (e.g., a community-based intervention that incorporates family process). While each of these have an important basis, the focus here will be on a family-centered intervention that has considerable promise as an agent of change for adolescents who have initiated substance use – the Family Check-Up (FCU). The FCU – developed by Thomas Dishion and colleagues – has not only been shown to reduce substance use in high-risk youth but in fact may have the most impact when directed at the most problematic youth and families most in need of services (see, for example, Dishion et al., 2013; Fosco, Frank, Stormshak, & Dishion, 2013). A number of similarly promising family-based interventions are also available in the field, but we will focus on the FCU as a prototypical method.

Why is the FCU an interesting example of a psychosocial intervention given the orientation of this chapter? First, the FCU is rooted in a developmental model that spans from childhood through adolescence. As such, it maps on well to the developmental orientation with respect to trajectories of substance use and the changing mix of genetic and environmental influences. Second, the core feature of the FCU is a focus on improving key parenting skills – particularly effective monitoring and limit setting – that have been shown empirically, in many studies, to be highly implicated as risk factors for initiation of substance use in adolescence. So this orients us to one stage of the "two-stage" genetic epidemiological model – initiation and early use of substances.

Third, deficits in core parenting skills that are the focus of the intervention are believed to inappropriately facilitate peer and sibling influences on early onset and use of substances – processes that are consistent with the contagion model that appears to mediate some of the shared environmental effect on adolescent substance use as well as CP. For example, poor parenting monitoring facilitates youths affiliating with delinquent peers and escalating their own CP. Within these peer groups there is not only exposure to substances but also a social climate that provides social reward for use. Similarly, the FCU has been shown to impact sibling collusion, or attempts by siblings to undermine parental control and facilitate rule-breaking behavior between siblings – a dynamic that increases the likelihood of problematic levels of both CP and SU.

The family-based framework is certainly consistent with the idea of aiming at social processes that have been shown to be reflective of shared environmental effects. In terms of the themes of this chapter, it should be appreciated that the FCU is ideally suited as a psychosocial intervention with potential impact on initial use of substances. In terms of direct effects, we would predict that it would not, for example, be as effective in reducing escalation from moderate levels of use to regular use (since this transition may be much more highly reactive to genetic effects rather than environmental influences). Such a matching of a psychosocial intervention with a developmental genetic epidemiological model demonstrates the complementary nature of these lines of work.

At this point, it is hoped that it is appreciated by intervention scientists and practitioners that there are potentially important layers of convergence between the rationale and execution of psychosocial interventions, and the etiological models offered by genetic epidemiological studies. But more than that, we now have a number of intriguing pieces that can be put together that may suggest how psychosocial interventions can serve to potentially block the activation of genes connoting additional streams of risk for youth – a particularly interesting way in which psychosocial interventions take on increasing meaning in the postgenomic era.

The intersection of the psychosocial intervention perspective and the genetic epidemiological framework demonstrates and anticipates a novel direction for future work. When we think of finding implications for intervention from genetically informative studies, we often reflect on the utility of tailoring interventions to high-risk groups. The idea would be that once we understand which youth are at high genetic risk, we could orient interventions to them. The ideas in this chapter, however, suggest two interesting alternatives.

One alternative is that the targets of psychosocial intervention could, in principle, negate the importance and impact of the individual differences in risk conveyed by having particular risk alleles without knowing anything about which genetic markers are implicated. For illustrative purposes, let's take this to the extreme. Let's imagine that the FCU could eliminate use of substances in adolescents who had initiated substances and begun to engage in sporadic use. If we take an extreme view of the developmental genetic epidemiological model, we would hypothesize that activation of systems of risk genes would not occur and the related negative impacts on the maturing adolescent brain would be circumvented. In this case, a psychosocial intervention would be completely effective in "preventing" gene expression, but it would be unnecessary to actually target specific risk genes – in fact, they could remain anonymous and the intervention would still work as long as it reduced and ideally terminated adolescent substance use.

A second alternative is that future intervention science could begin to incorporate genetic markers into clinical trials. Note though that this is different from saying that genetic markers would be used to *tailor* interventions toward high-risk youth based on measured genetic risk. Rather, the idea is that interventions could provide "microtrials" (see Howe, Beach, & Brody, 2010) – relatively brief and focused environmental manipulations – that offer many design advantages such as those derived from randomization offering a strong platform for examining genetically moderated sensitivity to immediate environmental change delivered by a psychosocial intervention.

This perspective draws on the now decade-long work on gene-environment interaction (GxE) in the developmental sciences. This research initiative has been cast in a very compelling manner because it is rooted in the idea that the environment may work differently depending on genetically influenced levels of susceptibility. The critically important conceptual point for intervention science is the idea that individuals may respond differently to the environment based on genetic differences. This idea has been reinterpreted by Jay Belsky and his colleagues as differential susceptibility to the environment, with genetic differences representing the degree of plasticity in response to environmental influence (see, for example, Belsky & Pluess, 2009). In this approach, genes are seen not as a potential diathesis (as has been the classic model), but rather as an indicator of likelihood of responsivity to the environment. The key clinical concept is that the *youth who are most likely to respond poorly to environmental risk factors may also be the ones who would respond most robustly to positive environmental influences*, such as those delivered via intervention.

Building on this idea, there have been forward-looking recent studies that have shown genetic moderation of preventive intervention effects on youth risk behaviors. Focusing on the serotonin transporter gene, a specific family-based intervention (the Strong African American Families program) has been shown to reduce a number of risk behaviors in adolescents at higher genetic risk, as compared to youth at genetic risk who do not receive the intervention (see Brody, Beach, Philibert, Chen, & Murry, 2009). Importantly, given the theme of this chapter, reductions in substance use have been one such risk behavior that was differentially reduced via intervention in adolescents with the "high-risk" allele. These findings reported in these papers are consistent with both the heightened attention given to gene-environment interaction (GxE) as well as the differential susceptibility perspective. What should be most appreciated by intervention scientists and practitioners is that psychosocial interventions may currently offer opportunities to examine directly how adolescents with putative high genetic risk for substance abuse and dependence may be particularly and positively reactive to environmental attempts to change their behavior (Brody et al., 2013).

SUMMARY AND LOOKING AHEAD

Stepping back from the various points of this chapter, what are the especially important messages for intervention science? First, there should be a sense of energy that comes from the multiple converging perspectives that argue for the importance of psychosocial interventions aimed at reducing risk for both CP and SU, as informed by compelling data from a number of genetically informative studies. The content areas targeted by many of the leading and empirically supported family-based psychosocial interventions are the very processes that are being shown to mediate the critically important shared environmental effect on CP and SU. And we are seeing in the literature theoretical models and empirical studies that bring genetics into psychosocial interventions in order to examine how these approaches may specifically benefit youth at high risk for risky behavior including substance use. Taken together, this is an exciting time for clinicians who deliver psychosocial interventions for CP and SU. Much of the enthusiasm comes from considerations of how psychosocial interventions may, in the future, prevent the development of genetically mediated problems – including substance abuse and dependence and severe and persistent adult manifestations of CP – by providing a developmentally timed, and environmentally delivered, blockade to gene expression. As such, there is reason to believe that our growing knowledge of genetics should be used as a platform for supporting psychosocial interventions as the fundamental approach for reducing risk for CP and SU. But to be maximally effective, we will need the type of commitment from funding agencies that recognizes why psychosocial intervention may be, in some cases, the most promising public health approach in the postgenomic era.

REFERENCES

Belsky, J., & Pluess, M. (2009). Beyond diathesis stress: Differential susceptibility to environmental influences. *Psychological Bulletin, 135*, 885–908.

Brody, G. H., Beach, S. R., Hill, K. G., Howe, G. W., Prado, G., & Fullerton, S. M. (2013). Using genetically informed, randomized prevention trials to test etiologically hypotheses about child and adolescent drug use and psychopathology. *American Journal of Public Health, 103* Suppl 1, S19–S24.

Brody, G. H., Beach, S. R., Philibert, R. A., Chen, Y. F., & Murry, V. M. (2009). Prevention effects moderate the association of

5-HTTLPR and youth risk behavior initiation: Gene X environment hypotheses tested via a randomized prevention design. *Child Development*, *80*, 645–661.

Burt, S. A. (2009). Rethinking environmental contributions to child and adolescent psychopathology: A meta-analysis of shared environmental influences. *Psychological Bulletin*, *135*, 608–637.

Burt, S. A., Klahr, A. M., Rueter, M. A., McGue, M., & Iacono, W. G. (2011). Confirming the etiology of adolescent acting-out behaviors: An examination of observer-ratings in a sample of adoptive and biological siblings. *Journal of Child Psychology and Psychiatry*, *52*, 519–526.

Burt, S. A., McGue, M., & Iacono, W. G. (2010). Environmental contributions to the stability of antisocial behavior over time: Are the shared or non-shared? *Journal of Abnormal Child Psychology*, *38*, 327–337.

Dishion, T. J., Breenan, L. M., Shaw, D. S., McEachern, A. D., Wilson, M. N., & Jo, B. (2013). Prevention of problem behavior through annual family check-ups in early childhood: Intervention effects from home to early elementary school. *Journal of Abnormal Child Psychology*, *42*, 343–354.

Fosco, G. M., Frank, J. L., Stormshak, E. A., & Dishion, T. J. (2013). Opening the "Black Box": Family check-up intervention effects on self-regulation that prevents growth in problem behavior and substance use. *Journal of School Psychology*, *51*, 455–468.

Howe, G. W., Beach, S. R., & Brody, G. H. (2010). Microtrial methods for translating gene–environment dynamics into preventive interventions. *Prevention Science*, *11*, 343–354.

Klahr, A. M., McGue, M., Iacono, W. G., & Burt, S. A. (2011). The association between parent–child conflict and adolescent conduct problems over time: Results from a longitudinal adoption study. *Journal of Abnormal Psychology*, *120*, 46–56.

Marceau, K,. Humbad, M. N., Burt, S. A., Klump, K. L., Leve, L. D., & Neiderhiser, J. M. (2012). Observed externalizing behavior: A developmental comparison of genetic and environmental influences across three samples. *Behavior Genetics, 42*, 30–39.

McGue, M., Zhang, Y., Miller, M. B., Sasu, S., Vrieze, S., Hicks, B., Malone, S., Oetting, W. S., & Iacono, W. G. (2013). A genome-wide association study of behavioral disinhibition. *Behavior Genetics, 43*, 363–373.

Moffitt, T. E. (1993). Adolescence-limited and life-course-persistent antisocial behavior: A developmental taxonomy. *Psychological Review, 100*, 674–701.

Rende, R., Slomkowski, C., Lloyd-Richardson, E., & Niaura, R. (2005). Sibling effects on substance use in adolescence: Social contagion and genetic relatedness. *Journal of Family Psychology, 19*, 611–618.

Rowe, D. (1983). Biometrical genetic models of self-reported delinquent behavior: A twin study. *Behavior Genetics, 13*, 473–489.

Rowe, D., & Gulley, B. L. (1992). Sibling effects on substance use and delinquency. *Criminology, 30*, 217–234.

Slomkowski, C., Rende, R., Novak, S., Lloyd-Richardson, E., & Niaura, R. (2005). Sibling effects on smoking in adolescence: Evidence for social influence from a genetically informative design. *Addiction, 100*, 430–438.

CHAPTER

5

Depression: The Importance of the Family as a Context for Gene Expression

Depression – particularly major depressive disorder (MDD) – is common. The lifetime rate of MDD is often estimated to be at least 15%. One in three women will experience an episode of depression in their lifetime. An especially vulnerable age period for women is the child-bearing – and child-rearing – years. This means that many children are exposed to parental MDD at some point during their youth – and also would presumably be at heightened genetic risk for depression. The start point of this chapter is to frame our discussion on depression in youth by deliberately setting up this idea that depression is highly familial and that the family is the most influential contextual risk factor for MDD. This is an easy perspective to support given the decades of study on offspring of depressed parents – and more recent intriguing findings that shed even more insight on the links between parental MDD and childhood behavior. But before we delve into that, it's worth stepping back and considering why the family has proven to provide particular insight into risk for MDD.

Looking at depression through the lens of this book is somewhat different than our approach to most of the other disorders discussed thus far. Autism spectrum disorder (ASD), attention-deficit/hyperactivity disorder (ADHD), and reading disability (RD) are all assumed to originate early in life and are thought of as childhood disorders – and the same argument can be made for conduct problems (CP). The bigger point is that our conceptions of these disorders are based on principles of early childhood development and require reference to deviations from normative patterns of social, behavioral, and cognitive development. In contrast, depression was historically conceptualized as a disorder experienced by adults with the reference point being changes in regulation of mood, cognition, and somatic functioning. Applying these criteria to youth has always been a challenge, posing theoretical as well as practical questions. Think about an adult who is in the middle of a severe depressive episode. They may suffer such a deep sadness that writers have described it as a "black hole." Thought processes get distorted, resulting in extreme guilt and feelings of worthlessness and hopelessness. Risk for suicidal thoughts and attempts may be heightened. Basic functions like sleep and eating may be severely disturbed. Anxiety may be profound. Someone who is in this state may show considerable psychosocial impairment, not being able to work or maintain social relationships. Some individuals literally find it extremely difficult to get out of bed.

It's hard to think that children would meet criteria of this nature – and how we would assess it reliably. While the field has found that MDD criteria can be applied with some clinical utility to teenagers – and such early onset of MDD shows an especially pernicious course – it is worth considering that our conceptualization of depression is still rooted in adulthood. Here's an exercise to make this point concrete. Diagnostic criteria reflect, in a fundamental way, what a clinician would think of as a prototypical patient. Think about the symptoms of ASD – and you will undoubtedly picture a young child, probably a toddler. Think about ADHD and RD – and you will conjure up the image of a school-aged child. But when you think about someone with MDD, an adult will come to mind.

Now of course depression in children – and adolescents – has been studied for decades using alternative methods, primarily via application of questionnaires that collect information on symptoms of depression that can be more age-graded. There has been much work on the cognitive and affective markers of risk for depression in school-aged children. These kinds of studies are important and extend our knowledge about the precursors to MDD – and the types of developmental risk experienced by some children. But a particularly important insight comes from examining the children of depressed parents and following them over time. This approach provided a unique window into the developmental trajectories of youth who were presumed to be at high risk for MDD – and also revealed the impact of growing up with a depressed parent. We will consider this in more detail.

HIGH-RISK STUDIES OF OFFSPRING OF DEPRESSED PARENTS

Long before the completion of the Human Genome Project (HGP) – and the dominating presence of molecular genetic research in the behavioral sciences – there was a hierarchy of how genetic studies of psychopathology would unfold. First, there needed to be sufficient evidence from family studies – classic examinations of family history and direct assessment of family members – to support the idea of familial transmission of risk. If there was no evidence of family "loading," there would be no need to even consider genetics (with respect to heritable genetic processes) as a relevant contributor to risk for a disorder. Once familial aggregation was established, then genetically informative designs – like the twin study approach – could be used to get a sense of the relative importance of genes and environment. If a number of studies supported the idea the genes may be relevant, then it would make sense to initiate molecular genetic studies.

It's useful to consider this hierarchy given the rampant assumptions that genes have to play a role in every disorder. While probably true, the collective mindset focuses immediately on DNA, and can obfuscate the critical point that it is important to understand genetic effects because many disorders are highly familial in origin. Similar to our discussion of CP, some clinically relevant constructs have an extremely strong familial basis and aggregate highly in family members. Our broader goal is not to then say we need to understand genes – what we need to do is study families as a primary context for risk for the disorder, understand the mechanisms that promote familial aggregation, and then consider the types of interventions that would be best supported by our understanding of process.

Such is the case with depression. Much of the historically important work that shaped our understanding of depression came from family studies conducted decades ago. These showed that MDD was highly familial – particularly MDD that had an early onset. Such was one of the contributions of Myrna Weissman and her research team in the 1980s. They provided compelling evidence that age of onset was a clear marker for familial aggregation of MDD – with earlier onset having a near dose response association with familial loading (see Weissman et al., 1984). It also became clear that onset of MDD in the teen years was not only highly familial – it also predicted recurrence patterns through adulthood. Hence, "early-onset recurrent depression" became a powerful clinical subtype of MDD that carried much predictive power in terms of a lifetime of increasing risk for depressive episodes that would increase in severity and impairment, along with shorter recovery periods.

Weissman's attention to early age of onset also led her to direct a spin-off of the family study: the high-risk paradigm. Her group took the platform of the family study – which typically focused on adults – and initiated studies of the children of depressed mothers. Importantly, these studies evolved into longitudinal investigations that tracked offspring from childhood through adulthood, providing unprecedented insight into the risk pathways for children at familial risk for MDD (see Weissman et al., 2006, for a perspective derived from two decades of study). From the diagnostic perspective, it was revealed that they indeed are at heightened risk for MDD during adolescence and adulthood, with corresponding high levels of impairment. In childhood, they are especially likely to show evidence of anxiety disorders, as well as other behavioral problems such as CP. More recent studies have confirmed that nearly 40% of youth with a depressed parent experience some form of clinically significant behavioral and/or emotional problems.

What can we extract from these critically important studies that have been conducted across decades? Well, we certainly know that there is "vertical" or intergenerational transmission of risk for MDD and related psychopathology. The risk unfolds in multiple ways in childhood, with problems in multiple domains of emotional and behavioral development. The onset of MDD occurs later in development, typically in the teen years – and predicts not only recurrence but also other clinical concerns such as substance abuse and anxiety disorders. So from a phenotypic perspective – without referencing the mechanisms underlying vertical transmission – growing up with a depressed parent is a strong marker of risk for a compromised developmental pathway, starting in childhood and continuing through adulthood.

We know that such transmission can be due to genetic influences, environmental effects, or a combination. So our next step is to consider what we have learned from studies to date that can inform our models of genes, environments, and gene–environment interplay to get a sense of what type of interventions may be useful.

GENETIC MODELS OF MDD

A variety of approaches have been used to examine the etiology of MDD, with the vast majority conducted with adults. As this body of work informs our understanding of depression in youth, it is instructive to consider the main themes that have emerged. A number of twin studies were initiated in the 1990s – a time when the twin method was applied intensively to psychiatric disorders – to examine the utility of the fundamental "biometrical" model that we have discussed in prior chapters. The typical finding was that MDD – defined according to standard diagnostic criteria – was moderately heritable. Typical heritability estimates would be around 40%. The remaining variance in the model was attributed to nonshared environment, as there was little evidence for shared environmental effects. Fair to say that most studies to date that have used twin modeling have come to this conclusion about MDD.

As we have seen, these basic biometrical models are start points, not end points. One of the ideas has been that MDD is a complex phenotype that might reflect a diverse set of conditions. For decades, there has been appreciation that there may be etiological heterogeneity underlying broad diagnostic disorders – that there may be, in essence, different causative pathways to similar clinical outcomes. As an example, recall that in Chapter 1 we referenced the idea that a small proportion of cases of breast cancer are due to major gene effects – whereas the majority of later occurrences presumably reflecting a more complex mix of multiple genetic and nongenetic factors. The same thinking has been applied to MDD, with the primary platform being the family study data described above that identified early-onset recurrent depression as a highly familial phenotype.

It makes sense that early-onset recurrent depression has been studied in the molecular genetic laboratory given the strong current of evidence that it is highly familial. Keep in mind, though, that there is not much evidence – for or against – the idea that early-onset recurrent depression is highly heritable. There have not been a series of convincing behavioral genetic studies that examined this subtype and compared the "etiological architecture" to that found for MDD that onsets later in life, or is not recurrent. This doesn't mean that the molecular genetic strategies are unfounded. But it's worth bearing in mind that simply knowing that a disorder or clinical phenotype is highly familial does not portend success in the search for genes, especially if there is not a straightforward pattern of familial aggregation that is consistent with a single or major gene model (for example, as is the case with Huntington's disease). It's best to assume that this work is exploratory, as is the case with nearly all forms of psychopathology.

Given this, it is perhaps not surprising that there are no established single or major genes for early-onset recurrent depression. The findings to date have suggested some genetic loci, but nothing beyond what we typically see for psychiatric disorders – more of an idea of the types of genes that may be involved rather than definitive statements about clear involvement of specific genes. Is it reasonable to assume that there are genes directly implicated in the etiology of early-onset recurrent depression? Of course it is. Is it troubling that such genes have yet to be identified? Not particularly – especially if we assume that there will be many genes involved that have relatively small impact individually. But what's salient is that it doesn't appear that early-onset recurrent depression should be thought of as a "genetic disorder" as we do Huntington's. The magnitude and patterns of familial aggregation tell us that – and given the power of genetic technology – if it were a single-gene disorder, it's quite likely that it would have been identified by now.

So how should we think about early-onset recurrent depression? Well, the easy answer is to cast it in the same light as nearly every other disorder. It's a complex disorder (meaning that there is not a singular cause), undoubtedly polygenic (meaning more than one gene involved), and probably reflective of additive genetic effects (numerous genes of small effect that add up to contribute to risk or liability). Given everything that we know about complex disorders, there must also be room for significant environmental effects in the model. Referring back to the modeling that's been done on MDD, we have seen that "genes" account for less than half of the model, with a healthy portion of variance residing in the nonshared environmental category. This construct has always posed some vagaries and challenges. Part of this component is assumed to be measurement error that reduces the ability to see the genetic signal (so that the calculated heritability may be a lower bound, rather than upper bound, estimate). Other contributions are assumed to be environmental influences that are unique to individuals, as compared to systematic shared environmental factors that operate to make family members similar. But these can be thorny to find.

The fact is that while the biometrical modeling of MDD and the familial and molecular genetic data on early-onset recurrent depression have contributed much to our understanding of the etiology of depression, the information yield doesn't suggest much right now in terms of implications for intervention with adults – or with youth who are at risk for developing MDD. More traction can in fact be gained by complementary strategies that have taken a different view of how genetic influences may operate for depression – particularly by overtly considering how the environment may have an extraordinary impact that can't be easily discerned in the biometrical model or in the molecular genetic laboratory unless it is directly assessed.

GxE INTERACTION AND DEPRESSION

Arguably the most influential paper published over the last decade in the behavioral sciences made just that point about the environment and genetics. In 2003, Avshalom Caspi and Terrie Moffitt (and colleagues) presented a framework for examining GxE interaction in general and as applied in particular to depression (Caspi et al., 2003). In particular, Caspi and Moffitt launched a methodological shift that is worth considering in some detail, as it has spurred an extraordinary amount of research on depression as well as other forms of psychopathology.

Back in 2002, it was becoming clear that it would not be easy to find replicable effects of single genes on psychopathology. A shift in thinking – probably over a decade in the making – was taking hold in terms of consensus that most psychiatric disorders were not due to single or major gene effects. So the goal was to establish a role for specific genes as contributors to risk. One approach that was influential (and still is) was to test out associations with candidate genes – genes that were known (or thought) to be expressed in the brain and involved in generating a gene product that had a role in a meaningful biological process related to the disorder in question. The thinking was that while each of these may have a somewhat weak signal, using large informative samples would aid in their detection.

Caspi and Moffitt challenged this view by arguing that genes for depression (and other disorders and clinically meaningful traits) don't just summate to create an overall genetic risk. In contrast they suggested that many genes of relevance to complex behaviors are essentially dormant until they are stimulated by the environment, at which point they then respond by producing whatever gene product they are responsible for. The key, though, is that people in the population have different polymorphisms (variant forms of the gene), which serve not to cause a disorder but in fact moderate the response to environmental influences (which in some cases will be maladaptive). In essence, their framework rejected the classic liability model in favor of the GxE interaction model by proposing that the types of candidate genes that are of interest to behavioral scientists and clinicians are fundamentally responsive to environmental stimulation – and make some people especially prone to a disorder as a response to environmental triggers, while others seem to be protected no matter what the environment.

Their approach was influential in a number of ways that reverberate today and as such deserve expansion. As described above, the conceptual framework caught on in a big way. Developmentalists have always found it more sensible to talk about nature and nurture – genes and environments – as acting together rather than separately. While main effects could be found for genes that impact behavior, these were limited to single gene disorders like Huntington's. Environmentalists always championed direct effects that were not impacted by genes – but could of course also acknowledge that the environment might have different effects on different individuals based on genetic propensities. Given the overwhelming interest in genes a decade ago, the GxE interaction model offered a very strong theoretical position that seemed timely (and still is) and could serve not just as a viable model but the preferred one for many forms of psychopathology that were assumed to not only be impacted by both genes and environments but more explicitly by their interplay.

But the influence went beyond a change in thinking. Caspi and Moffitt demonstrated that it was possible to not just invoke the basic GxE interaction framework (which of course wasn't new), but in fact translate it into research paradigms that could include, as they put it, both "measured genes" and "measured environments." The implication was profound. Developmental researchers had always collected information about the environment. Those interested in genetics could now easily obtain biological specimens (like saliva) and send them out to laboratories to acquire genotypic data for candidate genes, given the advances in technology that made this approach not only feasible but affordable (in terms of budgets for research grants).

Influencing thinking and outlining new methodological achievements are certainly indicative of a paper with strong impact. But the Caspi and Moffitt paper went beyond that by showing strong evidence of GxE interaction with respect to life events and depression. Unpacking what they did might help explain their success. As described above, they took a candidate gene approach, and focused on the serotonin transporter gene (referred to here as 5-HTT). This choice made good sense for a few reasons. Clinical depression responds to drug treatments that in principle increase levels of serotonin in the brain (the class of drugs referred to as selective serotonin reuptake inhibitors). Prior studies of the 5-HTT gene had provided evidence that it moderated reactions to stress and anxiety provoking situations – those that were homozygous (had two copies) for the short arm (one of the polymorphisms) were at much higher risk than those that had one or no copies for the short arm.

Perhaps underappreciated was the fact that they honed into one of the core psychosocial predictors of depression in adults – life events. There had been a very long history linking exposure to life events and onset of depression, and it was clear that stressful life events were one of the strongest predictors. So going beyond just measured genes and measured environments, this study examined a candidate gene and a "candidate environment" that had been shown for decades to be a core risk factor for depression.

Putting all this together, Caspi and Moffitt showed that while the 5-HTT gene was not predictive of depression (in their sample of over 1,000 adults) – or put another way did not have a main statistical effect – it strongly moderated how individuals coped with experiencing life events. Those that were homogeneous for the short arm were at much higher risk for depression in response to life events than all others – who in turn were much less likely to become depressed in the face of life events.

This paper has triggered a tremendous amount of research attempting to replicate and expand the findings. Such replication is important for an area of research but is especially so for genetic studies, as the possibility for chance findings are pronounced (given the expected statistical effects and the requisite sample sizes needed to generate sound estimates). Many studies provided evidence of GxE interaction with depression. Other studies did not report replication. Reviews of the studies and meta-analyses (joint statistical analysis of data from a number of informative studies) were conducted. The evidence for GxE interaction was hotly contested by some and debated in the literature. Ten years later, if you asked leaders in the field if they believe that the initial findings replicated, it may very well be that the answer would depend on who you asked.

Replication and debate are important features of the research world. But the drawn-out dialogue has obscured the bigger initial point of the original study that seems especially timely – that it is essential to factor in key environmental influences in order to understand better how genes operate. Any advances in methodology that would permit more robust findings that replicate would of course be welcome. But it is hard to dismiss the fundamental notions that episodes of MDD often occur in conjunction with life events and stressors – that is in fact a very old and supported idea in the clinical and epidemiological literatures – and the newer idea that some individuals may be especially vulnerable because of specific gene variants. Whether it turns out that the 5-HTT gene is indeed a key moderator in this process is not as important as grasping the broader conceptual point that searching for MDD genes without incorporating the environment may be a futile strategy.

DEPRESSION IN ADOLESCENTS AND CHILDREN

Given that our primary focus is to consider how risk for depression unfolds in childhood and adolescence – in order to consider appropriate intervention strategies – it's useful to consider the implications from the GxE interaction studies. There is in fact some evidence that 5-HTT interacts with stressors when predicting depressive symptoms in adolescents. But the bulk of evidence to date about the environment has suggested that it might have direct main effects (independent of genetics) during the teen years – much more so than in adulthood.

The studies that have come to this conclusion have not examined GxE interaction, but rather have used a twist to the basic biometrical model used in behavior genetics in genetically informative designs. The twist is to apply a method known as DF analysis, so named for John DeFries and David Fulker who developed the approach. Here's how it works. Many studies rely on measuring symptom levels of psychopathology rather than diagnoses, especially when studying children and adolescents. When this approach is taken in genetically informative samples (like the twin design), it is possible to examine if the estimated relative mix of genetics and environmental effects for the higher scores (meaning the youth with the highest levels of symptoms) differ from those found when the entire distribution is considered. Put another way, the idea is to see if the etiology of the extremes differs from the etiology of individual differences.

The interesting picture to emerge from a number of studies has been that extreme cases of depressive (children whose depression scores exceed a given cutoff) show strong evidence of shared environmental effects – a type of influence that is negligible when studying the full range of scores. This finding has been reported in studies that have used a variety of large, genetically informative samples in the United States and Europe, conducted across the last two decades (a good example is provided in Rice, Harold, & Thapar, 2002). A number of these projects (including the Nonshared Environment in Adolescent Development project and the National Longitudinal Study of Adolescent Health) have expanded the basic twin design to also include siblings of varying degrees of genetic relatedness, including full biological siblings, half-siblings, and biologically unrelated siblings that are growing up together. This is advantageous because there are some constraints when studying just twins – including the degree to which findings would generalize to non-twin siblings. The pattern of results has been the same with the data showing clear effects of shared environment that apply to both the twin and non-twin sibling pairs (see, for example, Rende, Slomkowski, Lloyd-Richardson, Stroud, & Niaura, 2006).

It should be recalled that, as discussed earlier in this book, substantial shared environmental effects were found for CP in adolescence, with a shift in influence changing in adulthood with the emergence of more impactful genetic influences. It may be speculated that the same kind of thinking can be applied to depression – with the exception being that the GxE interaction studies suggesting that the role of environment may be even more important during adulthood for depression as compared to CP.

Let's step back and reconsider all the models we have reviewed thus far. If we focused just on early-onset recurrent depression, the strong pattern of familial loading and the dose-response relationship between age of onset and familiality might seem to imply strong genetic effects with discrete ages of onset. In this case the model might look like the one that best explains Huntington's disease – there is in a sense a discrete clinical event (an onset), the timing of which is controlled by genes.

We know we don't observe the telltale patterns of familial aggregation when we look at the data on MDD. And we haven't found a genetic basis for it. Perhaps more importantly, unlike Huntington's, it appears that risk for MDD – especially early-onset recurrent depression – unfolds slowly starting much earlier in life. That's how the results of the high-risk studies can orient our thinking about developmental staging and the likely mechanisms involved. Children who grow up with a parent who has a history of early-onset depression are indeed highly likely to suffer the same fate when they become adults. But unlike Huntington's disease, they show clinical signs well before then via elevated rates of anxiety disorders and increased levels of emotional and behavioral symptomatology.

So the key issue here is whether these problem behaviors (recall that earlier a recent study showing that nearly 40% of children of depressed parents show clinically significant levels of diverse symptomatology) should be seen as the earliest manifestations of a genetic disorder, or rather reactions to a rearing environment that may be influenced to a lesser degree by genetic propensity. One line of evidence to bring into the mix here is the well-established finding that depressed parents can be quite compromised in terms of their parenting. Depression can lead to social withdrawal, which in the case of parenting can mean a parent may be emotionally unresponsive to their child. The negative thinking that can characterize a depressive episode may translate into excessive criticism of a child. In addition to sadness, a depressed parent can also be highly irritable, anxious, and hostile with a child. There is a very large literature that has documented these observations.

In some ways these types of parenting behaviors are similar to those observed as risk factors for CP. What's especially interesting is that a recent clever study suggested that the effects of parental depression on behavior problems in childhood are environmentally mediated.

In summary, there is a clear role for genes in the etiology of MDD in adulthood. Current thinking emphasizes, though, that genes may in fact reflect reactivity to the environment rather than a biologically driven process that is indifferent to context. The developmental pathway to depression, though, starts early and is influenced strongly by the environment – specifically shared environmental factors that place siblings at risk. We see in great detail that this pathway can involve a number of behavior problems – not just early emerging depression – which are highly sensitive to ineffective parenting. Thus, two conclusions may be offered at this point: intervention strategies aimed at reducing the early problem behaviors of children at risk for depression should be psychosocial in origin, and it makes sense to look within the family for clues on what needs to change.

WHO SHOULD BE TREATED IN FAMILIES AT RISK?

Not every person who develops MDD had a depressed parent. But the proportion of risk in the population is definitely skewed toward the familial nature of depression, especially for the most insidious form of early-onset recurrent depression. Anchoring our discussion of intervention around families – the framework endorsed at the beginning of this chapter – would certainly in principle apply to large portion of youth at risk for MDD.

Intervening with youth who suffer from high levels of depressive symptoms and related behavioral problems – and adolescents with an early onset of MDD – is not like treating adults. Adults with severe symptoms may respond well to any number of types and classes of antidepressant medication. Various forms of psychotherapy can also be effective. In some cases a combination of both approaches may be optimal. But the bottom line is that many adults with MDD can be treated successfully (though it may take some trial and error to find what works best). This isn't the case with adolescent MDD. Antidepressants tend to not work well with teenagers – and in some cases can make symptoms worse. As unambiguous manifestation of MDD in prepubertal youth is especially rare, it is also the case that there is not a sound empirical base to support pharmacological approaches. Adolescents with MDD can respond to psychotherapeutic efforts, such as cognitive behavioral therapy – though they are much less likely to experience improvement if they have a depressed parent. And children of depressed parents who present with a range of behavioral problems are not good candidates for pharmacology either.

So where does this leave us? The intriguing answer is that a key may be to utilize the treatability of adult MDD. Weissman and a group of collaborators made a critical observation in a large sample of adults undergoing treatment for depression. As expected from high-risk studies, the rates of psychiatric disorders and behavioral problems in the offspring (between 7 and 17 years of age) were extremely high. Nearly half of the offspring had a history of at least one psychiatric disorder – and substantial numbers had current symptoms. However, when parents responded well to treatment – when their symptoms lifted and their depression remitted – their children showed marked improvements as well, with corresponding reductions in behavioral and emotional symptoms (for example, Pilowsky et al., 2008).

What is especially intriguing is that a series of papers from this group have expanded these findings to suggest that these effects are not just transitory. Follow-up evaluations at 3-month intervals suggested that the effects were holding up – impressively even one year after initial assessment. The comparison of interest was children of parents who remitted (whether they responded to treatment immediately or more slowly) versus children of parents who did not respond to treatment. The offspring of remitted parents had significantly fewer psychiatric diagnoses, lower levels of behavioral problems, and better overall psychosocial functioning. Of note, behavioral problems increased in the children of nonremitters over the one year period.

What might be responsible for these findings? One finding to date is that when parents' symptoms remitted, their levels of warmth and acceptance increased. These are core dimensions of parenting that affect children on a consistent basis day after day. They are parenting behaviors that are known to be compromised in parents who suffer from MDD. And by successfully treating parents for MDD, warmth and acceptance improve without any other form of intervention or parent-based instruction. It's simply the lifting of severe symptoms of MDD that, in and of itself, can change how a parent interacts with their child – and in turns leads to stable decreases in offspring problem behaviors and symptomatology.

This body of work suggests a general psychosocial mechanism in which children's functioning – social, emotional, behavioral – mirrors the quality of parenting. As this process works in both directions – remittance of MDD in parents reduces children's symptomatology, and worsening of parental symptoms has a negative effect on their offspring – it is reasonable to assume that there is a high degree of reciprocity between parent and child, along with much plasticity. Judy Garber – who was a member of the research team that conducted the initial work described above – tested out these ideas in a fine-tuned way. Her team examined parents with MDD who were participating in treatment, and their children, six times over a two-year period, providing an opportunity to map out the degree of reciprocity between parental and child depressive symptoms. What they found (see Garber, Korelitz, & Samanex-Larkin, 2011) was quite striking and consistent with the research described above. Some parents responded well to treatment – whether it was psychotherapeutic, pharmacological, or a combined approach – and some did not. When parents showed improvement in their functioning and reduction in their depressive symptoms, so did their children – and this pattern was observed over the two-year period. Interestingly, if parents who remitted initially began to show increasing levels of depressive symptoms at a later time, their children's level of depressive symptoms followed suit – they went down, then went up, in parallel with their parents. And if parents did not improve despite being in treatment, their children showed a more pernicious course over the two-year period. It is worth noting that fathers as well as mothers were included in the study, and this pattern of reciprocity between parent and child were observed for both. While the sample wasn't large enough to adequately test for potential differences between mothers and fathers, it does seem that parental depression – and not just maternal depression – affects kids negatively but is malleable via treatment.

Garber's paper also converged with the prior work by showing that a key change in parental behavior that was associated with remittance was an increase in acceptance. Taken together, a key thing that happens when parents with MDD respond well to treatment is that they become nicer to their kids – they are more responsive, more affirming, and more affectionate. Such behavior seems to have a potent and immediate effect on their children.

IMPLICATIONS OF THE PARENTAL TREATMENT STUDIES

So what are the larger implications of this emerging body of research? There are many. First, a practical implication is that delivering effective treatments to parents with MDD may be the most powerful intervention we have for reducing the very strong risk for depression in their offspring. There is no other tested approach that yields both the immediacy and magnitude of the effect. We do know, however, that not every parent seeks out – or has easy access to – treatment. We have seen enormous research efforts devoted to understanding the genetics of MDD with some of the implication being that it will inform prevention as well as intervention. These approaches – while important for the scientific point of view – have offered no directives for reducing risk for depression in offspring. In contrast, from a public health perspective, an investment in initiatives that delivered and assessed the benefits of treating parents with MDD would provide an immediate reduction in risk in their offspring. This is an example of the type of prioritizing that has permeated research funding on MDD in general and psychopathology in particular. A decade after the completion of the HGP, we may have learned more about the psychosocial processes that underlie transmission of risk for MDD between parent and child rather than the genetics, along with a roadmap for providing immediate benefits to offspring at high risk.

To that end, there is certainly room for further refinement of this paradigm. We have just begun to see some of the changes in parenting that occur when MDD remits. Much more could be done to provide more insight into how these can be promoted and expanded – especially since there has not been any attention given to direct intervention with respect to parenting skills. If we learn more about this, it might provide some insight into bolstering the parenting skills of parents with MDD who do not respond to treatment. Remember that their offspring not only show high levels of behavior problems and elevated rates of psychiatric disorders, but also trajectories of worsening symptoms over time. It's worth considering that these parents may need a booster in terms of psychosocial interventions to try to reverse this trend – especially since the Garber work suggested that the linked escalation of depressive symptoms in parents and offspring may be bidirectional. Think about it this way. A parent with MDD with low levels of warmth and acceptance and high levels of hostility will promote these types of behavior in their offspring – which may further increase the levels in the parent. It becomes a vicious cycle that plays out in real time. But it is in principle reversible. The Family Check-Up (FCU) intervention – which was discussed in Chapter 4 in reference to both conduct problems (CP) and substance use (SU) in adolescents – has been shown to reduce levels of depressive symptoms in parents of toddlers (see Shaw, Connell, Dishion, Wilson, & Gardner, 2009). Part of the effect may be due to simply providing some social support to the parents. Another benefit may be empowering parents by helping them to develop more effective skills. And of course, part of the feedback loop is that better skills will improve child behavior, which in principle should benefit a parent's mood level.

The implication is that parents with MDD may be vulnerable to the effects of their behavior on their children, so that if they are able to learn and apply the skills offered in the FCU, it may improve their children's behavior and hence have some impact on reducing their own depressive symptomatology. This kind of study is relatively straightforward to design (examining, for example, the effects of administering the FCU, treatment for parental MDD, or a combination of both), but would need research support that may be hard to find in a climate that prioritizes genetic and biological strategies that have not produced any deliverables to date improving the developmental trajectories of offspring at high risk for MDD.

That last statement should also resonate when we reflect on the plasticity of behavior in the offspring. It's clear that the proximal (or immediate) psychosocial environment in the home has surprisingly immediate effects on them. While adult MDD – and especially early-onset recurrent depression – may appear on the surface to present like a genetic disorder with discrete breakdowns in functioning, the developmental roots are not like that at all. We know with certainty that early-onset recurrent depression doesn't just "onset" per se but is most typically preceded by prior behavioral and emotional problems including increases in depressive symptomatology in childhood. The emotional climate in early and middle childhood sets a template for distortions in cognition (like a negative attributional style) that are predictive of later onset of depression. All of these processes unfold in a complex way in interaction with the environment and are particularly sensitive to the disproportional influence of parenting. It's an open question how much of the vulnerability to MDD could be reduced by changing the early rearing environment of offspring at high risk. But it's a much better bet than thinking about tailored genetic interventions for genes that have yet to be identified much less understood.

All of these considerations do not imply that genetics are not important. Quite the contrary is true. What they suggest is that the more recent genetic models that overtly consider gene–environment interplay are on to fundamental truths about depression risk – disentangling the genetics of MDD from the environmental contexts that promote it may completely misrepresent what this disorder is all about. The diathesis–stress approach of Caspi and Moffitt may hold promise for understanding which children are at particularly high risk for being reactive to the behavior of a parent with MDD. The concept of differential susceptibility may provide insight into why the negative patterns of interaction – and reciprocity of depressive symptoms – between parent and child may also yield so easily to treatment and change so rapidly. These models of gene–environment interplay may guide how we follow genetically vulnerable children over time, and across developmental epochs, to see how far the reach of the early environment extends. And they may in fact aid the gene-chasing initiatives by focusing efforts on genes that function in response to the environment rather than being indifferent to it.

There could be a very large research agenda here. Some may argue that we have already seen a strong commitment to GxE interaction research on genetics, given the level of funding supporting it and the number of papers published on this topic. They may suggest that the net result has been debate and a lack of consensus and perhaps polarizing acceptance or rejection of the concept. So why continue in that direction? A reason to do so would be to cast these academic debates – which are important – within research strategies that can actually change children's lives right now. Even if we don't come to any conclusions about GxE interaction ten years from now, we would have valuable data on parents with MDD, their offspring, and the factors that help promote and sustain improvements in their functioning. Not everyone who suffers from MDD has a family history. Not every child at risk for depression has a parent with MDD. But in terms of focusing on a perspective that would identify a group at the highest risk for MDD, the family unit is a very strong one. It would certainly provide a platform for expanding our thinking about the genetics of MDD with respect to salient developmental periods and the earliest manifestations, and mechanisms, of risk. And it would build on a strong platform that reveals how modifying the psychosocial environment of youth who are presumed to be at the highest genetic risk for MDD may in fact buffer whatever vulnerability resides in their DNA.

REFERENCES

Caspi, A., Sugden, K., Moffitt, T. E., Taylor, A., Craig, I. W., Harrington, H., McClay, J., Mill, J., Martin, J., Braithwaite, A., &

Poulton, R. (2003). Influence on life stress on depression: Moderation by a polymorphism in the 5-HTT gene. *Science, 301*, 386–389.

Garber, J., Korelitz, K., & Samanex-Larkin, S. (2011). Remission of depression in parents: Links to healthy functioning in their children. *Child Development, 82*, 226–243.

Pilowsky, D. J., Wickramaratne, P., Talati, A., Tang, M., Hughes, C. W., Garber, J., Malloy, E., King, C., Cerda, G., Sood, A. B., Alpert, J. E., Trivedi, M. H., Fava, M., Rush, A. J., Wisniewski, S., & Weissman, M. M. (2008). Children of depressed mothers 1 year after the initiation of maternal treatment: Findings from the STAR*D-Child Study. *American Journal of Psychiatry, 165*, 1136–1147.

Rende, R., Slomkowski, C., Lloyd-Richardson, E., Stroud, L., & Niaura, R. (2006). Estimating genetic and environmental influences on depressive symptoms in adolescence: Differing effects on higher and lower levels of symptoms. *Journal of Clinical Child Adolescent Psychology, 35*, 237–243.

Rice, F., Harold, G. T., & Thapar, A. (2002). Assessing the effects of age, sex and shared environment on the genetic aetiology of depression in childhood and adolescence. *Journal of Child Psychology and Psychiatry, 43*, 1039–1051.

Shaw, D. S., Connell, A., Dishion, T. J., Wilson, M. N., & Gardner, F. (2009). Improvements in maternal depression as a mediator of intervention effects on early childhood problem behavior. *Development and Psychopathology, 21*, 417–439.

Weissman, M. M., Wickramaratne, P., Merikangas, K. R., Leckman, J. F., Prusoff, B. A., Caruso, K. A., Kidd, K. K., & Gammon, G. D. (1984). Onset of major depression in early adulthood. Increased familial loading and specificity. *Archives of General Psychiatry, 41*, 845–852.

Weissman, M. M., Wickramaratne, P., Nomura, Y., Warner, V., Pilowsky, D., & Verdeli, H. (2006). Offspring of depressed parents: 20 years later. *American Journal of Psychiatry, 163*, 1001–1008.

CHAPTER

6

Pediatric Bipolar Disorder: Complex Phenotypes, Genotypes, and Environments

Bipolar disorder (BP) has received intensive study by geneticists for decades for a number of good reasons. It can be a debilitating and beguiling disorder with potential for great impairment and harm. Manic episodes can lead to risky and deadly behavior. Severe depressive episodes not only carry their own pain and suffering but are associated with risk for suicide. Decades ago family genetic studies – including large "family tree" type approaches that collected information on generations within a family – established that BP has a strong familial basis. Twin studies consistently revealed high heritability estimates. These lines of evidence, combined with the severity of the disorder, made it seem likely that there was a fundamental genetic contribution.

In 1988, a published paper provided evidence that BP was due to a single gene. Around that time, another paper reported that a different gene was responsible for schizophrenia. These findings were on the heels of gene discovery for disorders such as Huntington's disease and seemed to portend breakthroughs based on genetics. The distinction between BP and schizophrenia was important because these disorders were thought to represent fundamentally different conditions and hence supported the diagnostic model used in psychiatry, which separated out distinct conditions with separable causes (historians will recall the phrase "Kraepelian" being used). So about fifteen years ago, it looked like bipolar disorder and schizophrenia were phenotypically distinct diseases that were due to different single genes.

CURRENT THINKING ON THE GENETICS OF BP

Since then, much has changed. It was recognized – rather quickly – that those initial findings were a bit shaky and required replication, which didn't happen. Many studies used the methods of gene discovery (linkage) to try to isolate better "the gene" responsible for BP and "the gene" underlying schizophrenia. Recall that this method has worked extremely well for single-gene disorders like Huntington's and cystic fibrosis. When it doesn't work – meaning it doesn't reveal a singular gene locus that is necessary (if you don't have the mutation, you won't get the disorder) and sufficient (if you have the mutation, you don't need any other risk factor to get the disorder) – the suspicion is that there is not a single gene at work. It could be that there is a major gene that doesn't fully explain the disorder but is a primary etiological factor, or that there is more than one gene involved. There could be some type of etiological heterogeneity – different types of causes that lead to the same disorder. Of course, the environment could play some type of role as well. The bottom line is that, after decades of intensive investigation, there has not been evidence of a single-gene etiology of BP – which in fact is consistent with the decades of family data that do not reveal specific patterns of inheritance characterizing diseases like Huntington's.

The thinking on the genetics of BP has changed dramatically over the years. Most importantly it is currently assumed that there are many genes of small effect size that contribute to risk for BP. While there have been some replicated findings of genetic association – meaning in essence a nonperfect correlation between a particular genetic marker and having BP – the genetic loci identified to date are assumed to reflect just a small portion of the genetic risk. This is a major shift in thinking that has occurred since 1988 when many in the field assumed that we would find a major gene.

Geneticists now clearly recognize and articulate the complexities posed by BP – not just at the genetic level, but clinically as well (see, for example, Craddock & Sklar, 2013; Domschke, 2013). There is much variety in the way that BP is expressed across individuals and those classic diagnostic boundaries may be fuzzier than previously thought. Of particular note is a strong current of research that suggests overlap between potential susceptibility genes that convey risk for schizophrenia and BP. That historical demarcation no longer seems to hold, both when family data are scrutinized and genetic data are examined. While there are still clear differences between schizophrenia and bipolar disorder, it is now accepted that the etiology of both is complex and connected to a degree – with some genetic overlap as well as assumed specificity (see Cross-Disorder Group of the Psychiatric Genomics Consortium et al., 2013).

In many ways, the etiological model for BP is similar to the one presented for attention-deficit/hyperactivity disorder (ADHD). It has been primarily conceptualized as a highly heritable disorder with a complex genetic and biological basis. Relatively speaking, not as much thinking has gone into considering a primary or key role for the environment. The complexities that are now acknowledged in the field – such as issues surrounding the specificity versus generality of risk genes and questions about diagnostic boundaries and phenotypic distinctions – reveal that we are witnessing a period of research that is, in part, redefining our fundamental understanding of the etiology of BP.

This brief sketch of the research landscape is critical because it provides the foundation for current thinking on pediatric bipolar disorder (PBD) – which is defined here simply as BP in non-adults (children and adolescents). And it serves to portend that we will be wrestling with even more complexity, and uncertainty, surrounding this construct.

IS PBD AN EARLY MANIFESTATION OF GENETIC RISK TO BP?

Before considering the issue of genetic influence, let's begin by briefly reflecting on how PBD is diagnosed. There are no developmentally unique criteria for PBD – in principle the same criteria used to diagnose BP in adults are applied when evaluating children and adolescents. There are no formal guidelines to guide a clinician through alternative manifestations of symptoms at different developmental periods. Clinicians of course use their judgment and developmental training to interpret the symptoms of bipolar disorder when evaluating youth, much in the same way that MDD is assessed in children or adolescents. This is not to say that this is a straightforward process. Over the past decade, there have been important studies that have brought together much clinical and diagnostic expertise to evaluate children and adolescents who are thought to suffer from PBD and track their clinical course. A good example is the COBY study (see Birmaher, Axelson, Goldstein, et al., 2009). Researchers at multiple sites across the country have been identifying and studying the clinical characteristics of children and adolescents diagnosed with PBD – and tracking their symptomatology over time. Part of the contribution is to identify the range of symptoms that may be observed – for example, some, but not all, show evidence of psychotic symptoms. A critical issue will be the longitudinal follow-up to see how many of these youth show evidence of BP when they reach adulthood.

What's most important here is the idea that researchers are in the middle of a very long process to both understand – and refine – the natural history of PBD and the developmental courses that can be observed in kids who are diagnosed with PBD.

Given that PBD is a viable clinical entity – meaning that it can be diagnosed reliably by experienced clinicians – we should be posed to discuss the genetic architecture of this disorder.

One perspective would be that PBD is an early manifestation of genetic risk to BP. In this model, it would, in essence, be the same disorder brought on by the same genes as adult BP, with perhaps some other factor influencing an early onset. Another possibility is that PBD is the result of unique genetic risk – either a higher "loading" or different genes.

There are, at present, no definitive answers to these questions. As discussed above, the thinking on the genetics of BP has evolved considerably over the last few decades – and there are no specific, robust genetic markers that can be held up as causative factors or as diagnostic indicators. So in one sense we are lacking information on BP that would help orient our perspective on PBD. Factor in that there have been no illuminating findings on the genetics of PBD and it is clear that we are far from answering the questions just posed.

This emerging picture on both BP and PBD landscape highlights the challenges raised, rather than answered, by the completion of the Human Genome Project (HGP). PDB – like BP – is defined by the constellation of symptoms, not by any type of genetic testing. To make this point concrete, if we were talking about Huntington's, we would say that this disorder can show a range with respect to age of onset. However, onset is always in adulthood, and individuals who carry the mutation typically don't start to show signs of the disease in their youth. If we were talking about cystic fibrosis, we would say that it onsets at birth, that multiple physiological systems are affected, and that the symptoms change over development. This progression of symptoms would be explained by the mutation. In both cases, we would be talking about a number of symptoms that get expressed at different developmental stages, which reflect the fact that genes can have their impact at multiple points in the lifespan (they don't necessarily have to "turn on" at birth) and can impact a number of biological systems (a principle known as "pleiotropy"). We do not have such benchmarks when studying PBD because we are not guided by the presence of a genetic mutation – it's not like we are trying to examine the developmental course of youth who have a known "disease gene." So it is premature to say, with respect to etiology, if PBD is BP emerging earlier in the lifespan, a subtype of BP, or in part a unique disorder. The lack of genetic markers that would permit answers to these questions highlights how the complexity of genetic influence has been illuminated by the completion of the HGP. The suspected strong impact of DNA is not going to be revealed so easily even for disorders like BP that we thought would be the ones most likely to yield to the power of the molecular laboratory.

Our need to learn more about the putative genetic etiology of PBD is underscored by the lack of quantitative genetic data in the literature. It was mentioned earlier that consistently high heritability estimates for BP, derived primarily from twin studies, were a strong impetus for searching for genes. To date, we have not yet seen seminal twin studies of PBD. Part of the reason for this is that PBD is not common. When crossed with the practical requirements of getting a representative sample of twins, it's difficult, in a pragmatic sense, to generate the large sample sizes favored in modern quantitative genetics with sufficient numbers of cases of PBD to generate meaningful estimates. But the issue goes deeper than that. As reviewed above, studies are still going on to carefully chart both the developmental course of PBD along with helping to define the clinical boundaries and phenotypic variations in subtypes of symptoms. Doing a twin study without a carefully defined phenotype is not maximally informative, and it makes sense that we have not seen large-scale efforts to date aimed at PBD.

With no genetic markers in hand, and no data from the quantitative perspective, our most influential information comes from the classic family designs to glean some insight into the familiality of PBD – that first step that historically had been taken before considering if genetic models need to be considered at all. One lens is application of the high-risk paradigm to examine the developmental profiles of offspring of parents with bipolar disorder, just as we saw this method used to look at patterns of intergenerational risk for MDD. A large high-risk study conducted by Boris Birmaher and colleagues (Birmaher, Axelson, Monk, et al., 2009) is worth looking at in some detail given the dearth of information on the genetics of PBD. This research team examined 388 offspring (between the ages of 6 and 18 years) of 233 parents with bipolar disorder as compared to 251 offspring of 143 control parents without psychiatric disorder. The offspring of bipolar parents showed highly elevated levels of PBD. The risk increased in families in which both parents had bipolar disorder versus families in which only one parent had bipolar disorder. These offspring were also likely to suffer from their first indication of a clinically significant mood disorder before 12 years of age, which is very young (as the most typical onset of a mood disorder is in the teen years). Taken together, these findings suggest some specificity of transmission of risk across generations – though not adherence to patterns of familial aggregation that would be consistent with a single-gene disease.

It is important to recognize, however, that the data are more complicated than that, perhaps reflecting what we have learned about the complex nature of the genetics underlying risk for BP. The offspring of bipolar parents also had significantly higher rates of any mood disorder, anxiety disorders, and other psychiatric disorders. Other research by Birmaher and colleagues showed that offspring of parents with bipolar disorder (again compared to community controls) who had not (yet) developed PBD had more severe levels of symptoms of multiple dimensions of problem behavior (including aggression problems as well as internalizing symptoms that include anxiety and depression). So while there is certainly evidence that risk for BP/PBD is transmitted from parent to child, it is also clear that these offspring show a variety of indicators of problem behavior in childhood and adolescence. It is worth noting that such complexity is introduced when the comparison is offspring of parents without any psychiatric disorders. It is not hard to envision that even less specificity of risk would be found if comparisons were made to offspring of parents with other psychiatric disorders (including MDD, anxiety, substance abuse, etc.) – the point being that what's most notable is risk for a broad range of behavior problems along with some specific risk for BP/PBD.

The high-risk method is just one window into patterns of familial risk and how it is expressed across generations. A complementary approach starts by identifying youth with PBD and then examining the rates and pattern of disorders in parents and other biological relatives. This method is called the "bottom-up" approach because it starts with offspring and then works upward in the family tree – in contrast to the high-risk or "top-down" design that starts with parents and then moves down the family tree to offspring. Bottom-up studies can also incorporate information about siblings (horizontal transmission) along with data on those "higher up" on the family tree such as parents (vertical transmission). To illustrate, consider a bottom-up study of PBD conducted by Janet Wozniak and colleagues (Wozniak, Faraone, Martelon, McKillop, & Biederman, 2012). They identified 239 children (between 6 and 17 years of age) who were diagnosed with PBD and conducted direct psychiatric interviews with 726 of their first-degree relatives (parents and siblings). In addition to a healthy control group, they also recruited 162 youth with ADHD and 511 of their first-degree relatives. While it is always informative to include a psychiatric control group – it helps us understand the degree to which patterns of familial loading are specific to a disorder versus signs of more general risk – the focus on ADHD is particularly useful because there is some overlap in the symptoms with PBD. For example, kids with ADHD and kids with PBD may have very high levels of impulsivity. In fact, there have been suggestions in the literature that such overlap is not just coincidental but rather reflective of common etiological influences. So including a control group of youth with ADHD but not PBD would permit assessment of the specificity of familial risk.

Wozniak and colleagues also incorporated data from published family studies of youth with PBD. On a technical note, they only considered data from research that used direct interview of each family member (the family study approach) by excluding studies that relied on family history (in which an informant from a given family provides data on other family members). This was done because the family study method is thought to be the most reliable way of gathering data on large numbers of family members. All of this is relevant because the combination of new data collection with such extraction from the family study literature provides a strong platform in terms of both numbers of families studied and the preferred methods.

After putting all these pieces together, it was suggested that there is strong evidence of elevated levels of BP in the first-degree relatives of youth with PBD. This pattern was significantly greater than that observed in families of youth with ADHD as well as healthy controls. Plain and simple, these findings dovetail well with the conclusions reached in high-risk studies as well as family studies of adults with BP – to a degree, there is a strong current of family risk for bipolar disorder as well as PBD. That said, other family studies show that while there is this specific risk, there is also an elevated level of other types of psychopathology in the families of youth with PBD. There can be increased rates of MDD, substance abuse including alcoholism, anxiety disorders, and antisocial behavior.

This mixed bag seems to be the rule rather than the exception for many disorders, not just PBD. As there are no specific genetic findings to reference with respect to PBD, we can only offer hypotheses that will be tested out in the years to come. As is the case with many psychiatric disorders, it's becoming more plausible to suggest that there may be "general" risk genes that convey vulnerability to a variety of disorders, along with some genes that are specific to disorders. This is hardly a new thought – the idea has been around for a long time and the general principle has been tested (and in part confirmed) in quantitative genetic studies of many disorders. What's newer, though, is empirical evidence at the genomic level of shared risk genes. For example, one provocative study reported that some genes are associated with risk for five psychiatric disorders (autism, ADHD, schizophrenia, BP, and MDD). Conceptually, this can make sense – there are just so many neurotransmitters residing in the brain, and just so many fundamental mechanisms underlying brain functioning that reflect expression of genes. Some of our genes may thus confer general risk (or protection) for a number of conditions. And then deep within that mix are the more specific effects that shape propensity for particular disorders. This emerging picture reflects a more complex reality for deciphering the genetic code responsible for classic disorders such as BP – and underscores the difficulties for finding "the gene" or genes that would be predictive of less understood conditions such as PBD. Given that, it's also understandable that we should temper our expectations about finding, anytime soon, tailored biological treatments as informed by genetics for PBD – especially as we don't even know, at this point in time, how heritable it may be.

THE CLINICAL COMPLEXITY OF PBD

So where does this leave us clinically? We continue to accumulate evidence that it is possible to reliably diagnose PBD. We know that youth with PBD show substantial impairment in multiple areas of functioning and certainly require intervention. But it is also fair to say that the diagnostic boundaries are quite fuzzy. Many kids may show a range of symptoms that might fall under the bipolar umbrella – or may reflect some other spectrum of dysfunction. As noted earlier, kids with PBD show symptoms that are consistent with ADHD. There are obvious parallels with MDD. Conduct problems, acting out, and temper outbursts may be observed. Age may be a critical factor, as it can be hard to decipher symptoms of mania in youth and differentiate them from emotional lability. We know that there is nothing in the biological laboratory – no genetic test or brain scan for that matter – that can be used right now to refine diagnosis and direct treatment. And while assessing family history can be useful, it is far from definitive in terms of making clinical sense of a child who is showing a range of symptoms that cut across a number of domains – emotional, social, and cognitive – especially when that family history can show familial aggregation of BP along with MDD, anxiety disorders, conduct disorder, and substance abuse.

The lack of clinical clarity – with no genetic or biological benchmarks to rely upon – is a somewhat sober reminder of where we are at nearly a decade after completion of the HGP. We have not used genetics to rewrite the diagnostic criteria for PBD or treatment protocols. As a result, we continue to have heated clinical debates about how best to serve youth who can show a baffling array of symptoms. This is best exemplified by a long process that has led to the inclusion of a new diagnosis in the 5th edition of the *Diagnostic and Statistical Manual* (*DSM*-5) of the American Psychiatric Association (published in May 2013) that arose out of the complexity surrounding how to best diagnose PBD – and the need to provide services to youth who don't meet the PBD criteria, yet are clearly impaired.

It is necessary here to devote some space to the *DSM*, as it illuminates where we are at – and where we would hope to be – with respect to diagnosis of disorders. The *DSM* is sometimes referred to as the "bible" of psychiatry, although this is an exaggerated misrepresentation. It is, in essence, a clinical manual that provides guidelines on the diagnostic criteria for psychiatric disorders. On the one hand, it serves as something of a consensus statement about how we currently conceptualize disorders – with the conditional "something" referring to the fact that committees are set up to formulate these consensus statements. At the same time, it stands as a very pragmatic codebook that is followed by most clinicians in order to provide a diagnostic label and code used to guide treatment and in many cases secure insurance payment for services rendered.

While beyond the scope of this book, it would be instructive to review how diagnostic criteria have changed over the last few decades – and how disorders get formally introduced into the *DSM*, how they get renamed, and how diagnostic criteria are revised (sometimes dramatically) over time. These changes reflect our ever growing empirical data base on the diagnostic process and natural history of disorders – and also our lack of gold-standard methods and measures that would permit diagnosis. Perhaps the nature of psychiatric disorders is that we will never have these. But again it's worth reminding ourselves that one of the goals of the HGP was to provide clarity derived from examining DNA that would solve these clinical conundrums. The promise was that well-studied disorders with a presumed fundamental genetic etiology like BP would be defined and diagnosed by analyzing DNA taken from blood or saliva. The hope was that subtypes of BP could be resolved by a similar process. The long-term goal was that PBD would be validated as a clinical construct via genetic analysis and differential diagnosis would be accomplished by examining a DNA report from the molecular laboratory.

In contrast, we have witnessed an elongated discussion – one that will be ongoing – about how to diagnose PBD and what to do about youth who show some of the symptoms but not enough to warrant a diagnosis. Focus here on the more practical aspect of the *DSM* – without a diagnosis a child or adolescent may not be eligible for treatment or qualify for needed insurance coverage to facilitate treatment. Here's the issue. You can think about a child who is suspected of having PBD as being unstable and explosive. Emotions may be extreme and unpredictable. There can be a lot of anger. Behavior may be difficult to regulate – there may be impulsivity and an inability to follow directions and rules. Cognitive functioning may be compromised, with inattention being prominent.

An experienced clinician will feel somewhat confident about sorting through this complex profile and use all available information to make a diagnosis of PBD, using the current criteria in the *DSM-5*. While there are no gold-standard methods available to "validate" this diagnosis, relying on clinical judgment is the best we can do. But the issue is as follows: What is a clinician to do if a given child is showing some of the symptoms of PBD but they don't add up to meet the diagnostic algorithm of the *DSM-5*?

This dilemma has resulted in a controversial decision – the inclusion of a new diagnosis in the *DSM-5*. This new diagnostic category – disruptive mood dysregulation disorder (DMDD) – was introduced in part (or, it could be argued, primarily) to help clinicians avoid overdiagnosing PBD, especially in children and youth who have not started puberty. The symptoms of DMDD are true to the name – they involve a mixture of both disruptive and undercontrolled behavior and difficulties regulating mood. Youth who would be diagnosed with DMDD exhibit persistent irritability and severe outbursts on a frequent basis (e.g., a few times a week). They have a persistent negative mood even when not having an outburst. There is an explosive element to them and a feeling (and reality) that they can erupt anytime and anywhere. Age is a key element in the diagnosis of DMDD – the bracket is younger than 10 years old and a chronological or developmental age of at least 6 years.

Why is this diagnosis controversial? For some, it represents the unfortunate tendency to put in place diagnostic categories without the requisite field testing. We are just seeing research papers coming out that look at the validity of the DMDD diagnosis – and particularly the utility of using this diagnosis to differentiate from other possible diagnoses like MDD, conduct disorder, and oppositional defiant disorder. We lack solid data on the stability of the diagnosis over time (e.g., Do kids "grow" out of it? Is it a marker for other diagnoses in the future?). Nearly every clinician who evaluated a child suspected of having DMDD would concur that this child is not developing well and is showing a number of troubling symptoms. But what these symptoms "mean" clinically would still be up for debate.

This is often the business of being a clinician who focuses on psychopathology in youth. But the bigger point here – in view of the primary theme of this book – is that we are still at a point where these debates are not informed by (never mind being resolved by) genetics. We have no genetic data to bring to the ongoing conversations about the pros and cons of DMDD and if it improves our ability to diagnose PBD with more specificity and rigor. Remember, this was one of the promises of genetic research in general. As described earlier, when the initial reports of localizing (via linkage analysis) the "gene" for BP in the late 1980s, there were papers published suggesting that the diagnostic process in general (and the *DSM* in particular) would be rewritten as a genetic manual. Current thinking is recognizing a more complex landscape for BP – both in terms of the number of genes that may be involved and the overlap of risk for many disorders (along with potential specificity for BP). We don't have genetic markers for PBD or even published estimates of the heritability based on genetically informative designs like the classic twin study. But given the current thinking on the complex etiology of BP, and the findings from top-down and bottom-up studies reviewed earlier (which echo both the idea of specificity along with risk for a broad range of psychopathology), it seems likely the PBD will be shown to have a similarly complex etiology.

EMPHASIZING PSYCHOSOCIAL INTERVENTIONS FOR PBD

The lack of genetic data on PBD and the complex etiological architecture of BP have been emphasized here for a reason – we still think of BP as not only a biological disorder but a genetic disorder. While this perspective is supported by foundational twin studies, the changing nature of how we think about the types of genetic influences argue that, like many diseases, BP is more likely a "complex" disorder in the etiological/epidemiological sense – meaning it is due to the influences of a number of genes, probable gene–gene interactions, environmental factors, and likely gene–environment interactions. The reality is that while attention has been given to the role of the environment as one class of causative agents for BP, research for decades has emphasized the biology and genetics of this disorder.

This mindset is critical when we look toward the best modes of intervention for PBD – and DMDD for that matter. Like BP, pharmacology is one of the options. For some this is worrisome – why treat with drugs when we don't know nearly enough about the biology of PBD? For others, it is a practical concern – managing a youth with PBD is challenging, their behavior can be dangerous for themselves and others, and every attempt needs to be made to manage their typically unstable moods and behavior. The same can certainly be said for DMDD.

There isn't a "right" or "wrong" here – it's a complicated issue with no immediate way of coming to a resolution. What we do know, however, is that we have much to learn about the pharmacology aimed at PBD. Victoria Cosgrove and colleagues (Cosgrove, Roybal, & Chang, 2013) point out – in an overview on the epidemiology and management of PBD – that we lack the requisite double-bling, placebo-controlled studies of medications used to treat PBD (such as lithium). It should be clear at this point that we are very far away from genetically (or even biologically) tailored pharmacological interventions for PBD, and for that matter BP. We continue to operate via drugs that have, in essence, shown to confer some benefit.

Partly with this in mind, it is critical to embrace another point made by Cosgrove and colleagues – psychosocial interventions provide feasible treatment options that are safe for youth. Furthermore, they are “evidence-based,” meaning that there has been accumulated and replicated empirical support for their utility as psychosocial treatments. These include the following:

Interpersonal and Social Rhythm Therapy for Adolescents (IPSRT-A)
Child- and Family-Focused Cognitive Behavioral Therapy (CFF-CBT)
Dialectical Behavior Therapy for Adolescents (DBT-A)
Family-Focused Therapy for Adolescents (FFT-A)

It is important to recognize that there are, as shown above, a number of psychosocial approaches that can be considered and used for youth with PBD. Of the interventions listed above, two themes stand out. First, most of the approaches are directed toward adolescents, which makes sense developmentally as they require a particular level of cognitive maturity. Second, some of the interventions are family-based, which speaks to the familial nature of PBD. The reality is that these are often used in combination with drug treatment. But the larger point is that they are part of the mix, and address the psychosocial climate of the family that may be observed when a youth has PBD – which provides a focus on the environment that has certainly not dominated the research literature but should receive much more attention in the future.

The importance of factoring in the psychosocial – and typically familial – context when treating PBD is illuminated by a study conducted by Miklowitz and colleagues (Miklowitz et al., 2008). They evaluated two treatment protocols for adolescents with PBD. One protocol combined pharmacotherapy with "enhanced care," which consisted of 3 family sessions that discussed relapse prevention. (This can be thought of as a standard treatment approach with a bit more emphasis on prevention.) A second protocol supplemented pharmacotherapy with the FFT-A (see above list of treatments). The FFT-A was labor intensive as it extended for 9 months. During those 9 months, a total of twenty-one 50-minute sessions were conducted – 12 weekly sessions, followed by 6 biweekly sessions, and concluding with 3 monthly sessions. The sessions included the adolescent patient, parents, and available siblings, thus being a truly family-based approach.

What kinds of unique therapeutic process occurred via the FFT-A? Three features were emphasized. Psychoeducation was used to provide a solid understanding of the symptoms of PBD, its course, and the environmental factors that precipitate recurrences (including life events and high levels of family conflict). This knowledge base was used as a platform for a second feature that emphasized recognition of early signs of recurrence – formalized as a "relapse prevention drill" via which such recognition would be translated into an action plan (such as facilitating an emergency psychiatric evaluation). A third component focused on supporting skills that would promote adherence with pharmacotherapy.

Did this extensive effort lead to more effective treatments? It did. Youth in the FFT-A condition recovered faster from their baseline levels of depression, spent fewer weeks in depressive episodes, and showed healthier patterns of depressive symptoms over a 2-year period. It's important to note that the study authors point out that future attention needs to be given to using FFT-A (and other forms of psychosocial intervention) to address symptoms of mania in youth with PBD.

This study illustrates what we typically see when we evaluate psychosocial interventions. They are not easy to administer, but they have positive effects – and no side effects. Family-based therapies can also be tailored to suspected psychosocial factors. For example, family functioning is often compromised when a youth has PBD. There can be many reasons for this. It may be that the behavior of youth with PBD is disruptive in the family – remember we are talking about children and adolescents who have intense negative moods, impulsivity, and difficulties regulating anger and controlling behavior. The family studies on PBD also suggest that the family climate may be an etiological factor in some cases, given the high levels of psychopathology that may be observed. Whichever way the causative arrows point, the bottom line clinically is that the family environment is a key factor that can influence the developmental trajectory of youth with PBD. For example, core features of family functioning – including adaptability, cohesion, and conflict – are often affected in families with a youth with PBD. As pointed out by Sullivan and Miklowitz (2010), these aspects of family functioning should be important targets for psychosocial interventions. And there is evidence that effective treatments such as the FFT-A work in part by influencing these types of processes. For example, in the treatment study described above, additional analyses revealed that reductions in family conflict partially moderated the treatment effect of the FFA-T (Sullivan, Judd, Axelson, & Miklowitz, 2012). Although these studies did not use a genetically informative design, it is worth considering that our prior discussion of conduct problems and substance use provided compelling evidence that family processes such as conflict have a strong environmental basis – and that psychosocial interventions may work via targeting modifiable behavioral patterns in families that are dysfunctional.

CONCLUSIONS

BP clearly has a biological basis. Genetics no doubt plays a fundamental role. But unraveling that role looks like a different challenge and enterprise than it did decades ago. It's becoming more and more likely that many genes are involved, only some of which are specific to BP. We have barely scratched the surface on the relevant environmental factors that operate independently of, and in conjunction with, risk genes. So while genes are arguably the core etiological influence on BP, deciphering how they have their effect will be as messy as it has been for many other "complex" disorders that involve multiple genes and putative environmental influences. This means progress will probably be slow (though the possibility of a breakthrough is always lurking in the background) and not necessarily steady. This is science. This is the science of complex human behavior and disorders. It's not an indictment of the field of genetics or the pace of discovery of genes.

It's simply the reality that we need to consider when we orient our research and treatment priorities for PBD. Even less is known about the etiology of PBD. Without question, there is a familial basis for it, no matter what angle we take when evaluating that issue (e.g., top-down, bottom-up). It's a complicated picture, both in terms of the range of disorders found in family members, and the range of symptoms shown by youth with PBD. It's not simple to diagnose, and attempts have been made to introduce other diagnoses that may prevent the overdiagnosis of PBD and permit better differential diagnoses. And, to state the obvious, we seem to be far away from using DNA to aid this diagnostic process and generate tailored treatments.

Should we continue to pursue those goals? Certainly. Should that pursuit dominate how we approach PBD? The argument here is that, when we take in the implications of all the points made above, we need to stimulate and prioritize the study and refinement of effective psychosocial treatments for PBD. We see the promise in some of the interventions that have been evaluated empirically. Many are designed for adolescents, leaving a void in the childhood years. This poses difficulties especially given the variable ways in which risk for PBD manifests during childhood. Many behavioral, emotional, and cognitive systems may be involved. Parenting skills need to be modified to deal with all this – and in some cases, this may require parental treatment given the substantial familial basis of PBD.

The likelihood that we are going to isolate a gene, or genes, with enough predictive power to generate tailored and effective pharmacological interventions for PBD that will substantially improve the natural history of the disorder seems, at this point in time, to be low. We need to be clear about why we are searching so hard for the genes underlying BP and question if such an approach will be warranted with PBD. Given that this scientific process seems to have a long future, the investment that would have the most immediate payoff for youth and families struggling with PBD would be improving our ability to deliver psychosocial interventions. These are not fast or easy and require trained personnel, extensive labor, and commitment on the part of youth and families. Recall the 9-month framework used to deliver FFT-A, as described above. They require both a conceptual and practical embracement by funding agencies and scientists alike. Consider the following. When we follow the debates about PBD – such as the one inspired by the inclusion of DMDD in the *DSM-5* – we eventually get to the point about discussing the pros and cons of medicating youth, particularly when the biological basis for those interventions are somewhat elusive with respect to specific processes and underlying pathology. The debates typically end there, with little spin-off into the need to support psychosocial interventions as the most promising and most important approach we need to take. No matter what we continue to learn about the biology and genetics of PBD, it is quite likely that will not change for a very long time.

REFERENCES

Birmaher, B., Axelson, D., Goldstein, B., Strober, M., Gill, M. K., Hunt, J., Houck, P., Ha, W., Iyengar, S., Kim, E., Yen, S., Hower, H., Esposito-Smythers, C., Goldstein, T., Ryan, N., & Keller, M. (2009). Four-year longitudinal course of children and adolescents with bipolar spectrum disorders: The Course and Outcome of Bipolar Youth (COBY) study. *American Journal of Psychiatry*, *166*, 795–804.

Birmaher, B., Axelson, D., Monk, K., Kalas, C., Goldstein, B., Hickey, M. B., Obreja, M., Ehmann, M., Iyengar, S., Shamseddeen,

W., Kupfer, D., & Brent, D. (2009). Lifetime psychiatric disorders in school-aged offspring of parents with bipolar disorder: The Pittsburgh Bipolar Offspring Study. *Archives of General Psychiatry*, 66, 287–296.

Cosgrove, V. E., Roybal, D., & Chang, K. D. (2013). Bipolar depression in pediatric populations: Epidemiology and management. *Paediatric Drugs*, *15*, 83–91.

Craddock, N., & Sklar, P. (2013). Genetics of bipolar disorder. *Lancet*, *381*, 1654–1662.

Cross-Disorder Group of the Psychiatric Genomics Consortium, Smoller, J. W., Craddock, N., Kendler, K., Lee, P. H., Neale, B. M., Numberger, J. I., Ripke, S., Santangelo, S., & Sullivan, P. F. (2013). Identification of risk loci with shared effects on five major psychiatric disorders: A genome-wide analysis. *Lancet*, *381*, 1371–1379.

Domschke, K. (2013). Clinical and molecular genetics of psychotic depression. *Schizophrenia Bulletin*, *39*, 766–775.

Miklowitz, D. J., Axelson, D. A., Birmaher, B., George, E. L., Taylor, D. O., Schneck, C. D., Beresford, C. A., Dickinson, L. M., Craighead, W. E., & Brent, D. A. (2008). Family-focused treatment for adolescents with bipolar disorder: Results of a 2-year randomized trial. *Archives of General Psychiatry*, *65*, 1053–1061.

Sullivan, A. E., Judd, C. M., Axelson, D. A., & Miklowitz, D. J. (2012). Family functioning and the course of adolescent bipolar disorder. *Behavior Therapy*, *43*, 837–847.

Sullivan, A. E., & Miklowitz, D. J. (2010). Family functioning among adolescents with bipolar disorder. *Journal of Family Psychology*, *24*, 60–67.

Wozniak, J., Faraone, S. V., Martelon, M., McKillop, H. N., & Biederman, J. (2012). Further evidence for robust familiality of pediatric bipolar I disorder: Results from a very large controlled family study of pediatric bipolar I disorder and a meta-analysis. *Journal of Clinical Psychiatry*, *73*, 1328–1334.

CHAPTER

7

Pediatric Anxiety Disorders: The Intersection of Genes and Environments

Anxiety disorders are very common. In fact, they are considered to be the most prevalent psychiatric condition in childhood and adolescence. They can onset throughout the lifespan. Certain anxiety disorders, such as separation anxiety disorder and specific phobias typically emerge during childhood. Some, like social anxiety disorder and obsessive-compulsive disorder tend to onset in adolescence. Others, including generalized anxiety disorder and panic disorder, have a first onset in late adolescence or sometime in adulthood.

Anxiety disorders are of core concern to clinicians. They can be debilitating due to profound impairments in social, emotional, and cognitive functioning and hence compromise an individual's life across developmental stages. Adults may be unable to work and even leave their own home. Children may become avoidant of school or certain social situations. Adolescents and young adults may experience extreme distress and withdraw from school. Furthermore, there is evidence that children who experience an anxiety disorder will continue to suffer from anxiety later in life (about one third who onset in childhood do so) as well as other related problems including depression and/or substance abuse (it is also estimated that this developmental progression affects about one third of children with an anxiety disorder).

In addition to the clinical significance of anxiety disorders through the lifespan, this group of complex conditions deserves consideration because they illuminate many of the challenges we face when trying to integrate our understanding of genetics and experience in the service of devising effective preventions and interventions for children and adolescents. We begin with a consideration of some of the key themes that can be considered when we view the anxiety disorders through this lens. We then turn to a specific example of a potent psychosocial precipitant of anxiety disorders in youth – maltreatment – that illuminates the concept of epigenetics, which may become a dominant theme in future research on genetics. The conclusion will focus on the possibility that our emerging understanding of how the environment shapes expression of genetic risk may provide a strong platform that emphasizes the critical importance of early psychosocial prevention of anxiety disorders.

THE HETEROGENEITY OF ANXIETY DISORDERS: FOCUSING ON ANXIETY-RELATED BEHAVIORS IN CHILDHOOD AND ADOLESCENCE

One of the obvious complexities of studying the etiology of anxiety disorders is the sheer number of disorders that need to be considered. Although they are lumped conceptually under the umbrella term of "anxiety disorders," they are arguably a collection of separate conditions that have very different clinical properties. This poses both opportunities and challenges when we look at genetic models and consider the role of experience in shaping risk for developing an anxiety disorder or disorders. Behavioral genetic research with adults has come to the general conclusion that there are both genes to seem to predispose to a range of anxiety disorders, as well as "specificity" genes that convey risk for each of the separate anxiety disorders. It is noted that this work has utilized quantitative genetic modeling that does not identify any of these genes. Rather the biometrical models used are multivariate extensions of the "basic" twin model.

Insight into the etiological architecture of anxiety in childhood, through the lens of the quantitative genetic model, has come primarily from employing quantitative measures of anxiety-related traits rather than application of diagnostic criteria. There are two related reasons for this approach. First, although many of the anxiety disorders are not diagnosed until adolescence or adulthood, anxiety-related behaviors may be observed clinically in childhood and measured via questionnaire (typically using parental responses). This leads to a second rationale for this approach: in quantitative genetics, the assumption is that risk genes contribute to a liability (or propensity) for developing a disorder, typically in conjunction with relevant environmental factors. Putting these two thoughts together, the appeal of a developmentally informed measurement and analysis of anxiety-related behaviors is that it may get at the earliest phenotypic signals of liability to anxiety disorders. As we will see, this general strategy has yielded insight into some of the early emerging risk phenotypes for anxiety disorders that may reflect multiple genetic liabilities – some that are specific, and some that are shared across related traits.

Perhaps the best known, and validated, example of this strategy is the construct of behavioral inhibition (BI). BI refers to a tendency for withdrawal or distress in the face of novel situations, new objects, and in the presence of unfamiliar people. While it has some parallels with shyness when the reference point is reactivity to strangers, BI is a separable temperamental dimension because it captures, at a more general level, negative reactivity to the unknown. There has been substantial laboratory and naturalistic research done on BI for decades and there have been theoretical and empirical links made between BI and underlying neurobiological systems underlying fear and anxiety. While measured as a quantitative temperamental trait, in research studies young children are typically classified as showing high BI.

BI is of particular interest because it has been shown to be a replicated predictor of later onset of anxiety disorders. For example, children who are classified as BI are at substantially heightened risk for social anxiety disorder in adolescence and later onset of other anxiety disorders such as generalized anxiety disorder. The power of the longitudinal designs required to evaluate these kinds of associations should be greatly appreciated. Studies that offer this type of information need to invest in a decade or more of tracking and evaluating samples and as such the yield is notable. Given this, BI should be considered to be a robust indicator of temperamental risk for anxiety disorders that emerges (and can be measured reliably) in the early years of life.

From the point of view of genetics, the question that can be raised is if BI provides a clue as to the foundations of anxiety disorders. When we think of temperament, we typically conceptualize it as inborn. Decades ago, the idea was introduced that being heritable was a necessary part of the definition of temperament. There is certainly much literature that supports this proposition. That said, the magnitude of the heritability of temperamental traits in childhood is often more modest than would be assumed, as typical heritability estimates range somewhere between 0.20 and 0.50 (depending on the construct under study). BI has shown evidence of higher heritability, with estimates ranging more between 0.40 and 0.70 across studies. It may be concluded that, at this point in time, BI may be the most heritable temperamental trait that is associated with later anxiety disorders, though it is far from being fully driven by the effects of genes.

This discussion highlights an older concept in quantitative genetics – the idea of an endophenotype (reviewed, for example, in Rende & Waldman, 2006). Referencing the classic "liability model" introduced above, it's been postulated for many years that genetic risk for psychopathology would be best captured in underlying biological mechanisms that are more purely a reflection of genetic propensity for a disorder (which would, in principle, aggregate or interact with other nongenetic risk factors to more fully determine onset of a disorder). Phenotypically, identified endophenotypes would be better "targets" for genetic research because they represented the most direct effects of genetic variation in the population. Thus, while the etiology of anxiety disorders is undoubtedly complex (complex in the sense of being due to many genetic and nongenetic influences), the hope would be that identifying endophenotypes would greatly aid our ability to find connections between genes and risk indicators – and that such progress would not only clarify the role of genes but also inform diagnostics and prevention.

Although BI does not meet the strict definition of an endophenotype (e.g., we would expect extremely high levels of heritability), it is worth considering that the research attention given to it does represent significant progress in the spirit of the endophenotype approach. It is measurable, it is predictive of later anxiety disorders, and it is heritable. As such, it represents a solid developmental approach that is interdisciplinary and also offers clinical prediction, as well as a methodology for identifying children at high risk for later onset of anxiety disorders.

This general approach of looking at underlying indicators of risk for anxiety in childhood, typically in the form of anxiety-related behaviors, has led to speculations about key cognitive and behavioral processes that can be examined in genetically informative designs. As an example, Salum and colleagues (Salum, DeSousa, do Rosario, Pine, & Manfro, 2013) propose a focus on key cognitive processes in childhood and adolescence that underlie risk for a range of concurrent and future anxiety disorders. They lay out a conceptual model that posits these processes as intermediate phenotypes, that is, traits that reflect genetic risk for anxiety disorders. The model here also suggests that these cognitive processes reflect fundamental aspects of pathophysiology in brain mechanisms that convey the expression of genetic risk when combined with exposure to relevant (though unspecified) environmental influences. Five specific mental processes are offered and are quoted here as the wording is nicely descriptive:

1. Threat-Attention Interaction (a tendency for anxious children to automatically orient their attention towards or away from threats);
2. Threat Appraisal (a tendency for anxious children to classify and respond to neutral or harmless stimuli as if they are dangerous);
3. Memory and Learning Processes (a tendency for anxious individuals to learn different associations among safe and dangerous stimuli, as presented in fear conditioning and extinction experiments);
4. Social Evaluative Processes (a tendency for anxious children to become concerned about peer evaluation); and
5. Increased Sensitivity to Rewards (a tendency for anxious children to more strongly alter their behavior when trying to achieve rewards)

(Salum et al., 2013, p. S6)

While this framework is appealing, it should be emphasized that it provides a platform for guiding research, rather than a summary of findings concerning genetic liability to anxiety in childhood and adolescence.

There are other studies that have taken, broadly speaking, a similar strategy by measuring anxiety-related behaviors (rather than diagnosed disorders) in childhood within genetically informative designs and as such are illustrative of how research is moving forward in terms of understanding how genes predispose to pediatric anxiety. What's notable in this approach is the idea that many anxiety-related behaviors are not inherently "pathological" – they are not only common but are in fact normative. The risk is more quantitative, in the sense of the level being greater than a normative range, just as BI is a compilation of an extreme tendency toward distress and avoidance when presented with novelty and unknowns. For example, Hallett and colleagues (Hallet, Ronald, Rijskijk, & Eley, 2009) examined the "phenotypic structure" of anxiety-related behaviors in a large sample of twins when they were 7 and 9 years of age. They identified five classes (or factors) of anxiety-related behaviors at both ages:

1. Negative Cognitions;
2. Negative Affect;
3. Fear;
4. Obsessive-Compulsive Behaviors; and
5. Social Anxiety

Again, note that, in principle, all youth could show some level of each of these anxiety-related behaviors. Within the quantitative genetic model, the idea is to examine the extent to which genetics explains the range of symptoms observed in a population under study. The conclusions of the study provide a good representation of our current understanding of anxiety-related behaviors in childhood. First, there were significant genetic effects on all five anxiety-related behaviors (i.e., significant estimates of heritability). Second, by using multivariate models that considered all five anxiety-related behaviors, Hallet and colleagues demonstrated that some of the genetic effects were shared or nonspecific, suggesting some commonality in the genes that influence a number of anxiety-related behaviors. That said, there was also evidence that each of the anxiety-related behaviors was also influenced by specific or unique sets of genes (bearing in mind that this work did not identify genes but rather quantitative estimates of genetic influence).

These findings highlight the importance of genes as a contributor to a variety of anxiety-related behaviors in childhood. But it is also critical to emphasize that the genetic effects, while significant and robust, were not the only etiological factors to emerge from the quantitative genetic modeling. Shared environmental influences – factors that promote similarity within twins (in this classic twin design that compares the similarity of MZ and DZ twins) independent of genetics – were also significant for all the subtypes of anxiety-related behaviors. Perhaps more telling, these seemed to reflect a general influence on all of the anxiety-related behaviors rather than being specific to each factor. While this study did not measure any putative environmental influences, these findings do suggest that there may be persistent elements in the rearing environment that contribute to an overall tendency for anxiety-related behaviors.

Hallet and colleagues note that the shared environmental effects in this study were "small," whereas the genetic effects were "moderate." While true in the numerical sense, it is important to recognize that these shared environmental effects are typically detectable in studies of children and alert us to the idea that all the explanatory power is not just in DNA. Furthermore, nonshared environmental influences (a theoretical mix of environmental influences that are unique to each individual with other more random effects including error of measurement) were also present – again reinforcing that while genetic effects in these types of models are notable, they do not inherently dwarf the relative importance of the environment. It is also posited here that it may be more important to recognize that both shared genes and shared environment help shape anxiety-related behaviors rather than rank ordering their quantitative effects – simply because the effect sizes in a quantitative genetic model do not tell us what will happen if we attempt to intervene and modify the underlying risk. For example, while genes may be important, we may not have the tools to alter their effects (a statement that is certainly true as of now with respect to anxiety-related behaviors in childhood). We do, however, have methods that can be applied to intervene behaviorally. This point will be expanded later in this chapter. The critical takeaway is that while we see, and acknowledge, how genes influence anxiety-related behaviors, this does not mean that we should ignore environmental factors, or the potential to modify risk for anxiety via environmental routes.

There is also evidence that genetic and environmental effects may operate somewhat differently across time – and here the importance of shared environment is revealed in greater detail. Trzaskowski and colleagues (Trzaskowski, Zavos, Haworth, Plomin, & Eley, 2012) utilized the twin design to take a more fine-grained look at anxiety-related behaviors at ages 7 and 9, and particularly the degree of stability in the five traits described above. In general, all of the anxiety-related behaviors showed evidence of stability, although the stability was described as moderate (as correlations between ages 7 and 9 ranged from 0.45 to 0.54 across the behaviors). One of the advantages of quantitative genetic modeling is that the general framework can be applied not only to a specific phenotype (univariate modeling) and multiple phenotypes (multivariate modeling) but also to longitudinal data, such that evidence can be gathered on the extent to which genes and environment mediate the stability of phenotypes across time. In this study, this type of modeling was applied to the five anxiety-related behaviors at the two ages, offering a number of possibilities because time effects could be considered as mediators of stability for a given trait (homotypic continuity) and stability across traits (heterotypic continuity).

The results of these complex analyses were illuminating. For each of the five anxiety-related behaviors, genetic factors were a primary source of the observed continuity. One way to think of this is as follows. The model predicts one of the anxiety-related behaviors at age 9 in one twin from the same anxiety-related behavior of the co-twin at age 7. To the extent that genetics influences stability, this cross-correlation (across twins and across ages) will be higher for monozygotic twins as compared to dizygotic twins – and that is what Trzaskowski and colleagues found. Overall, they estimated that 68% of the homotypic continuity (continuity between the same measures of an anxiety-related behavior at two ages) was attributable to genetic effects.

A different and intriguing picture emerged for a shared environment. Recall that a shared environment was found to have a general effect on all of the anxiety-related behaviors with little evidence of effects specific to any of these traits (as described above from the Hallet et al. study). In the same vein, although shared environmental effects were not a major source of continuity for each specific trait, they contributed to the heterotypic continuity across different traits, especially the association between fear and negative affect. Trzaskowski and colleagues use this finding to speculate on the possible types of shared environmental influences that could be operating. They bring particular attention to parental factors, including parental control, parental perception of fear, and negative affect. Complex designs would need to be used to test out the idea that these types of parenting traits are indeed "environmental" influences – but the bigger point here is that we continue to see a potentially important role for shared environment with respect to anxiety-related behaviors. Based on the data to date, these may be of substantial clinical significance because they appear to have a more global impact on the development of a range of anxiety-related behaviors, suggesting that some children are growing up in rearing environments that may promote a general propensity for anxiety.

ANXIETY IN THE FAMILY: THE INTERSECTION OF GENES AND PARENTING

The discussion of the role of shared environment for anxiety-related behaviors highlights a more general principle that anxiety runs in families. There is substantial evidence that parents and offspring show high levels of similarity for anxiety disorders and anxiety-related behaviors. Simply put, parents with clinical anxiety tend to have children who will also suffer from anxiety, and the converse is true in clinical practice – a child who is diagnosed with an anxiety disorder is likely to have a family history of anxiety disorders (see, for example, Salum et al., 2013). Of course, the driving force behind the twin studies of anxiety (and more generally genetically informative designs) is the assumption, borne out by family data, that anxiety is familial. The goal is not so much to figure out if this is genetic or not – it's clear that the anxiety disorders are "complex" disorders that involve the putative effects of multiple genes and multiple environmental influences – but rather to gain insight into the various ways that genes and environments may each play a role.

There is much interest in taking this perspective a step further by looking at specific mechanisms of interaction between genes and environment. A parent with an anxiety disorder conveys, in principle, both genetic and environmental risk for anxiety to their offspring. In nuclear families, it is very difficult to tease apart these influences and evaluate how they intersect to either promote or reduce risk for anxiety in offspring. A powerful window is to use the classic adoption design, particularly when data are available on biological parents as well as adoptive parents. Such is the approach of the influential Early Growth and Development Study (EGDS), a prospective longitudinal adoption study that collects data on adopted children, their adoptive parents, and their biological parents. The utility of this approach is straightforward (though of course there are many complexities to doing this type of study well): biological risk as represented in data from the biological parents can be crossed with environmental factors (the adoptive rearing environment) that are not confounded with genetic risk. It thus offers a unique naturalistic way of seeing how genetics and environment come together in development.

The EGDS team has provided insight into the intersection of genes and environment with respect to risk for anxiety disorders in the first few years of life. It is worth presenting an overview of the methods used because they highlight how the adoption design can still yield, in this age of genomic research, critically important information on genes and environment. As noted above, the EGDS recruited "adoption-linked families" – meaning that the study was able to assess adoptive parents, biological parents, and the adopted children. The adoptive families were available to be studied as a family unit, permitting insight into their family dynamics and rearing environment. This is an important point, as detailed observational methodologies could be used to collect data on the children, parents, and parent–child interaction. Such rich ecologically sensitive data provide a state-of-the-art assessment of behavior and parenting that are not always included in genetic studies of parents and children. Assessments were made early in life and multiple time points were used to begin to track development over time.

With respect to risk for anxiety, an EGDS paper by Natsuaki and colleagues (Natsuaki et al., 2013) provides an elegant example of thinking through how genes and environment may intersect. Attention was given to assessing the lifetime history of social phobia (SP) in 275 birth mothers. While such family history data may seem out of date, it is worth emphasizing that, for most psychiatric disorders, family history remains the most powerful predictor of risk to offspring (particularly given the lack of diagnostic or prognostic genetic markers). It is certainly something of a proxy for genetic risk – but it in fact takes on more significance because this putative risk is separated out from the rearing environment.

This is where the adoptive parents come into play. The EGDS team focused on maternal responsiveness, a construct that has been researched extensively and has been shown to be an influential element of parenting in general, with specific implications for risk for anxiety. Responsiveness encompasses social, emotional, and behavioral elements of parenting. Highly responsive parents show high levels of positive affect, and are especially attuned to their child's needs, providing appropriate and contingent responses. Prior work suggests that anxious parents tend to be less responsive to their children, with the speculation being that the lack of contingency provides one stream of environmental influence that promotes fear and inhibition in the early years in life.

With a proxy for genetic risk available, and detailed observational measures of rearing environment (adoptive mothers' responsiveness), analytic methods could be used to examine the main effects of each as well as the interaction of these two factors (a form of assessing gene – environment interaction or GxE). Given the young age of the offspring, the EGDS team focused on measures already discussed in this chapter: behavioral inhibition (BI). While prior discussion focused on the possibility of BI being an early manifestation of genetic risk for later anxiety disorders (particularly social anxiety), here the question is reframed as examining if BI reflects the intersection of genetic risk and environmental influence.

The results reported in Natsuaki et al. (2013) supported the idea that BI is a product of interaction between genes and environment. Offspring of biological mothers with a lifetime history of BP (and thus assumed to be at genetic risk) did indeed show increased BI at 27 months – but it was dependent on the responsiveness of the adoptive mothers. If maternal responsiveness was low at 18 months, then the offspring at familial risk for anxiety had higher levels of BI. But if maternal responsiveness was high at 18 months, the levels of BI were not elevated.

Naturalistic designs such as the adoption paradigm used in the EGDS are certainly not perfect (Natsuaki and colleagues provide a good overview of the limitations and caveats). But they continue to offer unique insights into the ways in which genetic risk may, or may not, be expressed in rearing environments by offering naturalistic teasing apart of nature and nurture. Taken together with the complementary perspectives offered by the twin research discussed in this chapter, the evidence to date suggests that the earliest manifestations of risk for anxiety clearly involve genes, environments, and their intersection. More pointedly, given the replicated reports of shared environmental effects, and the documentation of the effect of the adoptive rearing environment (with specification of maternal behaviors), it can be stated that multiple genetically informative designs converge on the conclusion that the social – and specifically familial – environment matters when addressing risk for anxiety disorders in childhood.

GENES, ENVIRONMENT, AND ANXIETY: NEWER METHDOLOGIES

Family, twin, and adoption studies are, relatively speaking, older methodologies. We've certainly seen why they continue to have a place in research today. But it's worth considering what we are learning from the newer methodologies, particularly those that utilize the modern methods of genomics. Before doing so, it's instructive to consider what type of operational genetic model we have for the anxiety disorders, particularly those that arise in childhood and adolescence. At this point in time, there are no big surprises here. Taken individually, each anxiety disorder is presumed to reflect moderate genetic influences, due in principle to the effects of multiple genes. There is clearly some role played by the environment for the range of anxiety disorders, though in many cases specific environmental "causes" remain elusive. In childhood, there is accumulating evidence that shared environment is significant. And we are seeing initial evidence that genes operate in conjunction with environments that can either promote or suppress risk for anxiety-related behaviors.

This general landscape can be used to offer three perspectives on the utility of conducting genomic work on pediatric anxiety disorders. First, there is clearly a reason to do so. All of the evidence to date, gathered via quantitative genetic modeling of data collected from a variety of genetically informative designs, points to an important overall role of genetic risk. That said, since the heritability estimates are typically in the "moderate" range, and given the absence of familial data suggesting evidence of major gene effects, identifying replicable gene markers for anxiety will be a potentially daunting (though not impossible) task. Finally, there is good reason to assume that as potential genetic markers are identified, they would be put to good use via combination with environmental measures. This is not new thinking, but rather a snapshot of the reality of where we stand with anxiety disorders in general, and pediatric anxiety disorders in particular.

The challenges of identifying genes for anxiety in childhood are well illustrated by the first study to search the genome for genetic variants associated with anxiety-related behaviors in childhood (Trzaskowski et al., 2013) as part of the Twins Early Development Study (TEDS) – one of the key studies referenced earlier that has provided evidence of the heritability of these traits. One of the advances in genomic research has been the development of techniques that search the entire genome for genes with small effect sizes (rather than searching for "disease" genes like those found for disorders like Huntington's disease). The approach – Genome-Wide Association (typically referred to GWAS for Genome-Wide Association Study) – is of particular interest because it provides a comprehensive search across the genome for the type of genes that are assumed to impact most (if not all) behavioral and emotional disorders. Put another way, we have seen, over the last few decades, that alternative strategies such as linkage (which is suitable for rare, major gene effects) and the candidate gene approach (which focuses on determining the degree of association between variants in a specific gene and a behavioral or clinical phenotype) have not delivered much in the way of replicable findings for the anxiety disorders and related traits.

Given all this, the Trazaskowski et al. (2013) report is notable both for providing a conceptual and analytic framework for the future as well as the initial findings. In addition to the application of GWAS, it is important that the focus is on anxiety-related behaviors that have been studied in the TEDS from the quantitative genetic perspective and shown to be at least moderately heritable (and thus influenced, as least theoretically, by a number of genes of small effect sizes).

Furthermore, GWAS requires relatively large sample sizes. Thus, it is notable that the TEDS sample for this study included data from 2,810 7-year-olds in an initial "discovery" phase (in order to reveal associations of interest) as well as data from 4,804 additional children also drawn from the TEDS (in order to replicate initial findings, a critical step in GWAS).

The findings are illustrative of the challenges posed by complex traits like anxiety-related behaviors. Over 700,000 genetic variants (single-nucleotide polymorphisms or SNPs) were considered. Overall, there was insufficient evidence of replicable associations given the SNPs that were considered. A method called Genome-wide Complex Trait Analysis (GCTA) was employed that can provide an estimate of the percentage of variance in the anxiety-related behaviors are explained by the SNPs (in other words, how well the genetic variants can account for the range in level of anxiety-related behaviors in this sample). These ranged from 1% to 12% for the anxiety-related behaviors.

This work by the TEDS team is highlighted for a number of reasons. First, it demonstrates newer genomic strategies that are geared to what we assume to be the most viable genetic model for anxiety-related behaviors – the accumulating influence of many genes of small effect sizes. This approach will bear watching as a methodology for examining the genetics of anxiety in future studies. In addition, Trzaskowski and colleagues provide a thoughtful consideration of some of the specific issues to be considered when examining childhood anxiety using GWAS and GCTA. For example, they note that the quantitative genetic studies could potentially provide inflated estimates of heritability – or that GCTA could underestimate the total effects of genes. They also pose the idea that alternative genetic models could be more appropriate for anxiety-related behaviors (such as models that emphasize interactions between genes or genes that have disproportionately larger effect sizes). The careful articulation of all of these possibilities offers an elegant exposition on the challenges involved in studying the genetics of complex traits like anxiety-related behaviors. The speculations do not mean that gene discovery won't happen – but rather than it will require dedicated effort and that the eventual yield may not be a certainty.

The GWAS approach, particularly as exemplified by the recent efforts of the TEDS group, will certainly be a relied upon methodology in the future. In terms of other newer methodologies, research on anxiety also illuminates the importance of considering the combined effects of genes and experience. While there are undoubtedly underlying genetically mediated vulnerabilities for anxiety, it is also clear that many environmental experiences can also induce anxiety symptoms. The traditional GxE model suggests that the intersection of genetic propensity and environmental experience conjointly impact risk for anxiety disorders. An important extension of this framework, rooted in developmental biology, goes further by postulating that experiences may in fact stimulate maladaptive biological processes by changing how genes get expressed over time. This general concept of epigenetics has tremendous implications for understanding the links between adverse environmental exposure and lifelong risk for anxiety and as such will be introduced here.

A key example in the literature has come from examinations of adults with posttraumatic stress disorder (PTSD), one of the more debilitating anxiety disorders. While many environmental circumstances can lead to PTSD, a common precipitator is maltreatment in childhood (physical and emotional). Childhood maltreatment is a substantial problem with tremendous impact on individuals and society. Concurrent and prospective studies certainly highlight the diverse effects on children in terms of social, emotional, and cognitive development, with anxiety-related behaviors and risk for anxiety disorders being prominent. It may be speculated that childhood maltreatment is one of the most impactful environmental influences on children – and one reason for this is that it induces a number a stress-related biological responses that have been shown to impact a number of physiological systems, effects that manifest as risk for multiple disorders in the adult years (e.g., Danese, Pariante, Caspi, Taylor, & Poulton, 2007).

With respect to the themes of this chapter, the idea of epigenetics is critical because it suggests that the environment drives change in gene expression that "engraves" long-lasting biological marks, as described by Mehta and colleagues (Mehta et al., 2013). These researchers compared gene expression (via examination of a biological process called DNA methylation) in adults with PTSD who differed in terms of history of childhood maltreatment. As the technical details are beyond the scope of this chapter, it's worth quoting the take-home message from this paper:

> Our results imply that biological perturbations in individuals with PTSD who have a history of childhood maltreatment may systematically and meaningfully differ from those individuals with PTSD who do not have a

> history of maltreatment. These findings suggest that taking into account exposure to childhood maltreatment is of great importance in the search for and application of gene-expression and DNA methylation signatures as biomarkers for PTSD and other trauma-related disorders.
>
> (Mehta et al., 2013, p. 6).

While there will undoubtedly be much more research done on epigenetics in the years ahead, this study illuminates the idea that environmental risks early in life (particularly especially impactful ones like maltreatment) may have a cascade of adverse effects on development (and risk for a variety of anxiety-related behaviors and disorders) through the lifespan, and one mechanism underlying those effects is by changing how gene expression operates.

CONCLUDING REMARKS

This chapter has sampled a range of approaches that span some of the oldest paradigms in quantitative genetics (twin and adoption studies) to some of the most recent and forward looking (GWAS and epigenetics). Clearly all of these paradigms will have a role in the continued investigation of anxiety in childhood and throughout the lifespan. We now consider some of the implications for prevention from these illustrative findings.

Family studies have established that anxiety aggregates in the family. Quantitative genetic methodologies establish that genes play an important role in terms of overall vulnerability.

Genomic strategies are examining what some of these genes may be and the magnitude of their combined effect. That said, the critically important role of the environment also comes through from the body of research to date. Shared environmental influences on anxiety-related behaviors in childhood are significant and replicable. Application of the adoption design has shown how characteristics of the rearing environment can either promote or reduce risk for early indicators of liability to anxiety disorders in toddlers who have a putative genetic vulnerability. Epigenetic methods are revealing how environmental insults such as childhood maltreatment may not only interact with genes but fundamentally how they get expressed in a maladaptive way, leading to a lifelong biological process of risk for anxiety and other disorders.

Given this picture, it seems clear that a priority for research, and a clear avenue for prevention, would involve psychosocial efforts directed toward known and suspected contributors to anxiety risk. Identifying the many genes that might be responsible for the moderate genetic effects on anxiety-related behaviors (and disorders) will not happen easily – and even as that work progresses it's not at all clear that it will have immediate implications for prevention and intervention. Epigenetic effects do isolate specific biological mechanism underlying gene actions, but again moving from that information gain to therapeutics or prevention will be a murky process given that there is no immediate road map for achieving this goal.

In contrast, there are decades of research on psychosocial approaches to anxiety-related behaviors and disorders, and certainly much evidence of benefit. With respect to prevention, a useful window is provided by a review of efforts to prevent abusive and neglectful parenting (one key source of maltreatment of youth) by Bentovim and Elliot (2014). The logic for looking at this particular branch of research comes from the increasing evidence, reviewed above, that maltreatment may interact with genes (see Cicchetti, 2013) and in fact alter the expression of genes. Any prevention that can substantially reduce the likelihood of child maltreatment would certainly reduce one stream of genetic influence on lifetime risk for anxiety disorders.

Is there evidence that this is an attainable goal? Bentovim and Elliot analyzed 22 randomized control trials to extract the "effective practice elements" from clinical efforts to prevent the recurrence of abusive and neglectful parenting. This effort identified 47 effective practice elements that show promise as preventive strategies. They also gathered a group of practitioners to generate ". . . a 'menu' of evidence-based, step-by-step modular interventions targeting the profile of abusive and neglectful parenting and associated impairments of children" (Bentovim & Elliot, 2014, p. 1).

This effort is clearly necessary from the basic lens of prevention. We know that parental abuse and neglect is often a recurring insult in a child's life, and that it has immediate clinical impact along with associated risks through childhood, adolescence, and adulthood. The speculation here goes beyond this clinical picture to claim that efforts to develop highly effective preventions that reduce the likelihood of parental abuse and neglect offer more immediate power to lower risk of anxiety disorders than biological strategies that may be informed by genomic research. This is simply one example of this line of argument, but it is bolstered by the clear identification of a modifiable risk factor (one with a very large effect on development) in the rearing environment of children that is being linked to impacting the expression of genes. Pushing this line of research forward will be time consuming and demanding, and will require substantial levels of funding to do it on a broad scale. The same can be said for genomic research including epigenetic approaches. The difference is that the funding for that line of work will undoubtedly be in place, whereas the probability of such broad-scale support of psychosocial interventions can be doubted.

REFERENCES

Bentovim, A., & Elliott, I. (2014). Hope for children and families: Targeting abusive parenting and the associated impairment of children. *Journal of Clinical Child and Adolescent Psychology*, *43*, 270–285.

Cicchetti, D. (2013). Resilient functioning in maltreated children: Past, present, and future perspectives. *Journal of Child Psychology and Psychiatry*, *54*, 402–422.

Danese, A., Pariante, C. M., Caspi, A., Taylor, A., & Poulton, R. (2007). Childhood maltreatment predicts adult inflammation in a life-course study. *Proceedings of the National Academy of Sciences USA*, *104*, 1319–1324.

Hallet, V., Ronald, A., Rijskijk, F., & Eley, T. C. (2009). Phenotypic and genetic differentiation of anxiety-related behaviors in middle childhood. *Depression and Anxiety*, *26*, 316–324.

Mehta, D., Klenger, T., Conneely, K. N., Smith, A. K., Altmann, A., Pace, T. W., Rex-Haffner, M., Loeschner, A., Gonik, M., Mercer, K. B., Bradley, B., Muller-Myhsok, B., Ressler, K. J., &

Binder, E. B. (2012). Childhood maltreatment is associated with distinct genomic and epigenetic profiles in posttraumatic stress disorder. *Proceedings of the National Academy of Sciences USA* (early edition).

Natsuaki, M. N., Leve, L. D., Neiderhiser, J. M., Shaw, D. S., Scaramella, L. V., Ge, X., & Reiss, D. (2013). Intergenerational transmission of risk for social inhibition: The interplay between parental responsiveness and genetic influences. *Development and Psychopathology*, *25*, 261–274.

Rende, R., & Waldman, I. (2006). Behavioral and molecular genetics and developmental psychopathology. In D. Cicchetti & D. Cohen (Eds.), *Handbook of Developmental Psychopathology* (2nd edition). New York: Wiley and Sons.

Salum, G. A., DeSousa, D. A., do Rosario, M. C., Pine, D. S., & Manfro, G. G. (2013). Pediatric anxiety disorders: From neuroscience to evidence-based clinical practice. *Rivista Brasileira de Psiquiatria*, *35*, S3–S21.

Tzraskowski, M., Zavos, H. M. S., Haworth, C. M. A., Plomin, R., & Eley, T. C. (2012). Stable genetic influence on anxiety-related behaviors across middle childhood. *Journal of Abnormal Child Psychology*, *40*, 85–94.

CHAPTER

8

The Future: Why Psychosocial Intervention Will Matter Even More

Each of the previous chapters discussed disorders that emerge in childhood and/or adolescence. Each follows the traditional diagnostic categories to a degree, but also recognizes that there are especially strong etiological connections between some classes of behavioral/emotional domains. It seems natural to discuss attention–deficit/hyperactivity disorder (ADHD) and reading disorder (RD) together from the genetic perspective because they not only coexist frequently, but the etiological model for each is similar and in fact represents overlapping influences. The same viewpoint supports lumping together conduct problems (CP) and substance use (SU). In contrast, early-onset major depressive disorder (MDD) and pediatric bipolar disorder (PBD) – at this point in time – don't seem to be as strongly connected in terms of family history and genetics, though of course there is some etiological overlap. So one point to be gleaned from this is that our etiological models don't always abide by the typical clinical boundaries or current diagnostic formulations.

We've long hoped that genetic research would redefine clinical definitions and provide new "objective" methods for making diagnoses. For example, if someone is showing clinical signs of Huntington's disease, a genetic test can confirm the presence of the mutation on the disease gene. What we have seen for the disorders we've discussed in prior chapters is that this may never happen simply because there may not be "a gene" for any of them. If you consider the order in which the disorders are presented here – ASD, ADHD and RD, CP and SU, MDD, PBD, and the many anxiety disorders – it parallels the perceived likelihood of finding "the gene." For ASD, it's possible that we are discovering rare genetic variants that, in some cases, may have disproportionate effects on risk. The pathophysiology underlying this process still needs to be elucidated and the impact of the rare variants on the developmental course of ASD still requires validation. All that said, it's not clear – and perhaps not likely – that identification of rare variants will explain the vast majority of cases of ASD or account for the very large increase in the rate of ASD in the population. Researchers continue to search for powerful genetic markers of RD – genes that may in fact have at least major effects on risk even if they are not "the gene." Then again, while RD is believed to be highly heritable, it's not established or evident that major genes exist. The same goes for ADHD, CP, SU, and MDD; they have all been best described, for decades, as complex phenotypes reflecting the individual and combined effects of multiple genes and environments.

While bipolar disorder (BP) was one of the best candidates for genetic studies for decades, we see how recent thinking on genetics has acknowledged many complexities – complexities that apply to our understanding of PBD, especially since we are in a very early stage of understanding the genetic contributions to that disorder. The sheer number of anxiety disorders highlight the challenges of sorting through the more general effects of genes that contribute to an overall risk for any anxiety disorder versus those that are specific to certain types of anxiety.

So it is clear that more than a decade after the completion of the Human Genome Project (HGP), genetic findings are not fundamentally rewriting our diagnostic manuals by focusing on core causes rather than descriptive pictures of symptoms. Referring back to the discussion of BP, when the first reports of genetic linkage came out in the late 1980s, strong statements were made in the field – and in the journals – on how our entire diagnostic enterprise would be rewritten by genetic findings. The *DSM* (*Diagnostic and Statistical Manual* of the American Psychiatric Association) would in essence become a genetic manual overhauled by what we know about DNA.

While that perspective may seem more than overly optimistic now, back in the late 1980s it did not seem farfetched. Why? As discussed throughout this book, the idea was that psychiatric disorders were being conceptualized as single-gene diseases. And the excitement was fueled by successes in locating the genes responsible for disorders – it seemed natural to assume that such identification would lead to unraveling the effects of a given gene and point directly to the development of effective therapeutics and/or preventions. Note that two concepts were embedded here. First, genetics would be used to diagnose.

Second, genetics would be the key to developing new, powerful treatments.

It is not controversial to say that such a perspective has changed drastically over the last 25 years or so. Although gene identification became possible for disorders that are due to a single gene, it is now clear that the pathway to understanding the etiological processes is not so simple. Talk to someone who has Huntington's disease – or a family member of someone afflicted with this disease – and you will learn quickly that there is no cure or even a genetically tailored treatment. The same can be said for many other single-gene disorders – such as cystic fibrosis – as we continue to learn that single-gene effects can still be beguiling despite the extraordinarily sophisticated advances in genetic methodology.

A second fundamental shift in thinking has been the development of a consensus that nearly every disorder covered in the *DSM* (not just those that are diagnosed in childhood and adolescence) is a complex disorder, ultimately shaped by numerous genetic and environmental factors. Back in the late 1980s and early 1990s, it was still something of a hard sell to say that the single-gene approach was not going to be the method of choice to gain traction in psychiatric research. The linkage approach – the one that led to identification of "the gene" for many single-gene conditions – was held in much higher regard than the more nebulous association study method. We've seen since then that linkage is quite powerful, when a disorder is in fact due to a single gene. The "failure" of linkage as applied to the disorders covered in this book is of course not failure but rather a confirmation that these are not, in most cases, single-gene disorders. Strategies like association – whether the focus is on specific candidate genes or genome-wide approaches – certainly come with potential pitfalls and some statistical fuzziness, but they are conceptually more appropriate to the etiological models that generate the most consensus in the field.

So the question remains – what next? If most disorders involve the effects of many nondeterministic genes, environmental influences, and interactions between genes, between environmental factors, and between genes and environment, what will advances in etiological research yield in terms of shaping intervention? Will we see what was promised prior to the HGP – major breakthroughs that radically alter how we intervene via genetically tailored treatments? We might see profound advances in knowledge, and they may (or may not) sharply alter our intervention strategies.

FUTURE GENETIC RESEARCH AND THE CONCEPTUALIZATION OF DISORDERS

In the aftermath of the introduction of the *DSM-5*, much was said and written about the lack of progress made in fundamentally changing the diagnostic frameworks and methods. It's still a symptom-based approach that sticks to the classic disease categories and labels. One ongoing direction of research that may change this is the National Institutes of Mental Health's (NIMH) Research Domain Criteria (RDoC) project. NIMH is been promoting research that goes beyond the *DSM* and utilizes a more dimensionally based model that attempts to characterize – and study – clinical conditions and populations using underlying dimensions of functioning. These include a cascade of processes that underlie cognition, emotion, and social behavior. The idea is that many of the clinical disorders can be broken down into specific mechanisms of risk and dysfunction that cut across these fundamental dimensions of behavior.

The crux of the approach comes from using and generating research criteria for describing clinical populations rather than the default *DSM-5* diagnostic criteria. These research criteria are used to both stimulate new thinking and provide a platform for how diagnoses may be revamped in the future. Consider the following from a press release issued on May 13, 2013, from Thomas R. Insel, M.D., Director, NIMH, and Jeffrey A. Lieberman, M.D., President-elect, APA:

> Looking forward, laying the groundwork for a future diagnostic system that more directly reflects modern brain science will require openness to rethinking traditional categories. It is increasingly evident that mental illness we be best understood as disorders of brain structure and function that implicate specific domains of cognition, emotion, and behavior. This is the focus of the NIMH's Research Domain Criteria (RDoC) project. RDoC is an attempt to create a new kind of taxonomy for mental disorders by bringing the power of modern research approaches in genetics, neuroscience, and behavioral science to the problem of mental illness.
>
> The evolution of diagnosis does not mean that mental disorders are any less real and serious than other illnesses. Indeed, the science of diagnosis has been evolving throughout medicine. For example, subtypes of cancers once defined by where they occurred in the

body are now classified on the basis their underlying genetic and molecular causes.

It is important to see where this kind of approach may go – and what implications it may have for how we intervene for the types of conditions discussed in this book. It's clear that a system based on the RDoC goes beyond the *DSM* in a few ways. It embraces dimensional thinking rather than a strict categorical structure. It acknowledges that different "disorders" will have some shared symptoms along with underlying etiological influences. Indeed, the orientation is deliberately focused on drilling down to the etiological level and capture underlying processes. As a thought exercise, consider how this approach may inform our understanding of disruptive mood dysregulation disorder (DMDD) – the controversial new diagnosis in the *DSM-5* discussed as an "alternate" diagnosis for youth suspected of having PBD. It would certainly be a step forward to have systematic research evaluate youth with this developmental profile from a dimensional approach to characterize the cognitive, emotional, and behavioral symptoms as deeper processes. Will it change how we diagnose? That's an open question. But this line of inquiry would certainly move beyond debates that center only on the most observable clinical symptoms.

The RDoC approach will, without question, increase our understanding of every disorder discussed in this book. It may eventually refine our understanding to the point that it changes how we diagnosis these disorders. Even the very small step of merging together ADHD and RD and CP and SU in chapters in this book is in the spirit of the RDoC approach, because it was a decision driven by our emerging understanding of common etiological mechanisms. But there is still something to take on about the RDoC approach – where will it lead in terms of shaping new interventions?

If you examine examples of the RDoC presentation on the NIMH website and consider how it may be applied in research, you will note that it is heavily skewed toward biological approaches. This is not inherently misplaced – the premise is that nearly all complex behavioral phenotypes have a strong biological basis. Probing deeper into the biology – genetics along with other complementary methodologies such as neuroimaging – is necessary. In the RDoC, there is reference to the environment as well, primarily in terms of gene–environment interaction (GxE). But it is fair to say that the bulk of the research effort is aimed at the brain and genome, and not the environment.

So one reaction might be to say that the role of the environment needs to be taken on with greater emphasis in the RDoC model. Or put another way, other complementary research programs need to be initiated that bring the same type of depth to study of environmental influences. While that is true, there's a bigger point to consider – we run the risk of assuming that most behavioral disorders are inherently products of biology, which means that biology will be the pathway to intervention. If we are going to apply the RDoC framework to how we think about ASD or ADHD or PBD, it's hard to emerge from that exercise saying that the end result is going to tailored psychosocial interventions. But that's a perspective that we need to not only consider but embrace.

Why? Let's start with the argument made thus far in this book that psychosocial interventions play either a primary or fundamental role in the best treatment model for all the disorders discussed. We have no biological treatments for ASD. ADHD is primarily addressed by pharmacology but we know these aren't tailored treatments – and that psychosocial intervention is not only advantageous but perhaps necessary to ensure the best possible outcomes. RD is best treated by educational interventions. CP and SU are not biologically treated – promising psychosocial interventions exist and are shown to have success. Probably the most effective treatment for depression in childhood is treatment of parental MDD. And while pharmacology is a treatment of choice for youth with PBD, we are seeing how psychosocial interventions enhance clinical outcome.

With this laid out, let's walk through what might come out of application of the RDoC model. Let's take PBD as an example. It would be a tremendous achievement to reveal something about the genetic architecture of PBD. Based on what we are learning about BP, the RDoC approach sounds like the right way to do this, because there will be "nonspecific" genes along with genes that have more specific connection to PBD. We will know more about how these genes play out in terms of structural and functional neuroanatomy – with a deeper understanding of the cognitive and emotional processes that may be going awry developmentally. We may even learn a little bit (probably not as much as we should) about the environmental contributions to PBD – and how they interact with and influence the underlying neurobiology and genetics.

Does all this mean, though, that we will end up with some type of biological "magic bullet" treatment for PBD? It's hard to see how that's going to happen, since we are going to be trying to integrate so much information that undoubtedly reflects a whole cascade of probabilistic influences across different developmental stages and biological systems. Our best hope will be to use all this information to deliver more tailored environmental interventions that have real promise for changing and shaping the end products of all these influences – perhaps in combination with more tailored biological interventions as well. The more complicated the model becomes, the more we have to appreciate that all the solutions will not come from the wet lab.

But that doesn't mean that the advances in genetics and evolution of psychosocial interventions are dissociated from each other. It doesn't mean that we will rely more on psychosocial interventions only "until" biology delivers the "real" treatments. It means that there will be more fruitful ways in which genetic research and psychosocial intervention will be consolidated in the future. Some of the research described here has illuminated some of the ways we are seeing this happen.

GENOMICS MAY REFINE DIAGNOSIS AND POINT TO TAILORED INTERVENTIONS

It's unlikely that we will completely rewrite our diagnostic manuals based on genetic findings. That's not to say that genetics won't have an impact – or in fact has already had an impact. Take ASD as an example. In the *DSM-5*, there is one diagnostic category of ASD. This is a dramatic change from the past because Asperger's disorder has been dropped as a diagnostic category. Asperger's had been used to characterize higher-functioning individuals on the autism spectrum. Now level of functioning is one dimension that is rated clinically and there is only one spectrum that characterizes ASD. This change has been controversial. It's not clear if it's an improvement or a step backward. But it was certainly influenced by decades of family and twin studies, which led to broadening the classic definition of autism and shaped the boundaries of ASD. It may be that genomics will inform further refinements and either support the "lumping" approach (lump all clinical variations into one diagnostic category) or point the way to a more empirically based "splitting" into separable diagnoses. This will be especially meaningful if it brings some clarity to response to intervention. Recall that in the chapter on ASD it was mentioned that the promising Early Start Denver Model (ESDM) intervention seems to have the most pronounced effects on youth who are higher functioning. It may be that genomics will provide some insight into this topic as it is researched over the coming years. For example, we might ask if children with identifiable rare genetic variants are also those who don't respond as well to ESDM (this is simply an illustrative hypothesis). This would be useful information because the ESDM is intensive and administered over a period of years. If we have some type of biomarker that, at a minimum, simply predicts likelihood of benefiting from ESDM, it will help direct intervention efforts.

It may be that this type of role for genomics is a more likely outcome rather than radical advances in diagnosis. It would be important if genomics could be used to refine diagnosis of ADHD. We worry that many kids are diagnosed with ADHD inappropriately, and biomarkers would certainly reduce the likelihood of that happening. They would also facilitate identifying youth who would profit from treatments designed for ADHD. But, again, this is a hope, not an expectation. We don't have a good model that shows us how to identify enough of the genetic signal to apply it meaningfully in a predictive or diagnostic sense.

It does not appear that such advances will automatically lead to biological breakthroughs for the disorders considered. They might. But what we need to embrace with more conviction is the need to use genomic research to deliver effective interventions to youth who need them. Much of the emerging work coming from a genetically informed perspective is either identifying the possibility of environmental pathways or bringing into focus actual environmental mechanisms that can support intervention. For ASD, we are seeing a new appreciation of shared environmental influences. Though it's not clear what the sources may be, it is at least an indication that identifying them may lead to environmental strategies that may minimize the risk of developing ASD.

Let's consider other possibilities. We are seeing more thinking on the impact of the psychosocial environment on ADHD and how it may intersect with genetic risk. We know there are etiological overlaps with RD. We see interventions aimed at RD can help improve cognitive performance. Perhaps all of these pieces will intersect in the future with more tailored and targeted environmental interventions that have an eye of the etiological mechanisms underlying the comorbidity between ADHD and RD. Offspring of depressed parents are certainly at genetic risk for MDD – but treating the parents for MDD reduces the level of that risk. Can this model be extended to PBD? Will there be common etiologies that suggest more linkage diagnostically between the disorders – or will they be separate entities? If we step back and look at interventions being delivered right now for conduct problems (CP) and substance use (SU) in youth, we see a productive merger between evidence-based practices (like the Family Check-Up), their desired social targets, and the blossoming identification of these targets as part of the robust shared environmental effect on risk for both CP and SU. CP and SU clearly have some influence from genetics, and perhaps genomics may sort out subtypes that are more or less "driven" by genetic propensities. This may play out diagnostically years from now. But a very real possibility is that such work would lead to interventions that are tailored to such diagnostic refinements – and perhaps bring to treatment the principles and lessons of constructs such as differential susceptibility to the environment (which proposes the somewhat counterintuitive argument that youth at highest genetic risk also are those most likely to respond dramatically to environmental influence).

GENOMICS WILL LEAD TO EARLIER INTERVENTION

It's a hope – not an expectation – that advances in genomics will lead to earlier intervention. Even if genomics does not rewrite the *DSM*, having in hand predictive markers could play a tremendously important role for getting interventions in place as early as possible. There is a growing literature on early identification of ASD. Much of this work relies upon detecting early behavioral signs that are predictive of later ASD. It would of course be invaluable to have validated biomarkers – not because they will lead to biological treatments, but because they could provide an empirical platform for the earliest interventions. Given the promise of the ESDM, it is critical to think – as those who do this work do – of the potential advantages of devising a variant that could be initiated in the first months of life, when we might hope there would be even more plasticity in the responsivity of the developing brain. Many think the genetic underpinnings of ASD are manifested as disruptions in fetal programming – so if the environment holds the potential of reprogramming, starting that process as early as possible would be something to shoot for.

This kind of thinking can extend to any of the disorders under discussion here. We typically wait until a child is well into his or her school experience – 2nd grade – before we consider a diagnosis of RD. We know, of course, that the precursors to reading start much earlier in development. Genetic markers that could reliably indicate which toddlers are at high risk for RD could both stimulate more research on earlier interventions and make their delivery more precise. We see that kind of thinking in early intervention models for CP – though those have not been enormously successful. Might more knowledge about the genetics sharpen those efforts?

Of course the discussion moves us from intervention to preventive intervention. This is a grand hope in the behavioral sciences and the focus on much research. We've seen application of principles derived from genetically informative research infuse this field and lead to both conceptual advances and practical application. What we need to embrace is the idea that, if they occur, genetic advances in early identification may have their biggest impact by directing efforts toward the earliest environmental interventions.

GENOMICS WILL ACCELERATE THE DEVELOPMENT OF PSYCHOSOCIAL INTERVENTIONS

While the most important deliverable of genetic research, when applied to the disorders discussed here, may be to accelerate the development of more effective psychosocial interventions, there are barriers to consider. We have not had a grand effort (anywhere near the scope of the HGP) that has taken as its mandate to translate genomic research into environmental interventions, despite the tremendous growth in the study of gene X–environment (GxE) interaction in the behavioral sciences. The worry here is that as that field moves slowly – given the complexities of how to conduct it and the realities such as the need for large sample sizes – the momentum it generated will not necessarily infuse the development of future interventions.

That would be a grand mistake. We have gone from promises about genomics to expectations about genomics back to promises about genomics. It may be the nature of science that we issue, every decade, a statement about what we see as the light at the end of the tunnel another decade from now. Those decades add up to the lifetime of an individual with ASD, ADHD, RD, and so on. Those promises and expectations are no longer viable. They are goals and hopes. The biological work that goes into those efforts is important. But thinking that their payoff will be biological cures or even treatments seems very mystical right now. Psychosocial interventions often have benefits, even if modest. Linking those efforts with the grander emphasis on genomics would be a much more effective way to take what we learn about DNA (and for that matter the environment) and use it to change the developmental trajectories of youth who are either at risk for disorders or suffering from them.

WILL WE DISCOVER MAGIC BULLETS?

We still hear about the possibility of magic bullets. There is ongoing research on Down syndrome, for example, that is hoping to eradicate the genetic basis for that disorder. We hear about emerging treatments for muscular dystrophy that use a form of gene therapy. Will these initiatives ever lead to the type of success that was discussed in Chapter 1 based on the Philadelphia chromosome?

They might. It certainly makes sense to pursue these possibilities because there are known genetic causes for these disorders. They are, fundamentally, genetic disorders, as is Huntington's disease. It is logical and rational to say that we may be able to treat, or even cure, genetic disorders by attacking the genetic deficit biologically.

But every disorder reviewed in this book does not seem to function that way. Genes play a role – maybe in some cases a prominent role – but there are probably many of them and their distribution across individuals may not be systematic. Getting our arms around all that complexity and reaching in for the underlying mechanisms that can be manipulated biologically to achieve meaningful clinical change is a murky proposition. Yes, it may work – but why would we expect it to work, not just any time soon, but ever? If that code gets cracked, then we will all celebrate. Children's lives will change for the better. But we can't assume that day will come and we can't rely on a possibility.

Psychosocial interventions improve the quality of children's lives right now. Toddlers with ASD experience advances in social functioning and we have seen that their neural responsivity to the human face can improve as a result of intervention. Children with RD learn how to have more success in school and how to compensate for the challenges raised by their processing style. Parents can be taught strategies to help their children with ADHD manage their behavior better. The likelihood of early-onset substance use can be reduced. Youth with depressed parents show decreases in their level of depression when their parents get treated – and the parent–child dynamic changes for the better. We hope to see more advances in treating PBD, but there is evidence that psychosocial interventions improve clinical course. There are a variety of evidence-based practices for maltreated children that could offer protection against the lifelong physiological changes and consequent risk for anxiety disorders that result from exposure to trauma.

The conclusion here is that we need to prioritize psychosocial interventions as an essential part of the eventual therapeutic effort and not just efforts we put forth until magic bullets are discovered. Furthermore, it is postulated that our discoveries to come from genomics will be most effectively translated into clinical gains via integration with psychosocial interventions. Finally, while psychosocial interventions without reference to genetics certainly works, integrating advances in knowledge about how genes and environments intersect would provide emerging platforms for developing more powerful interventions that can initiate as early as possible in development.

As a final point, we should consider casting our genomic work within large-scale prevention and intervention efforts. These efforts could provide large samples, and the type of clinical, developmental, and biological information needed for genome discovery research are typically and/or easily obtained via the intervention study platform. Such a strategy would also offer response to intervention as a phenotype to be integrated with genomic markers, along with salient environmental mediators and moderators.

This approach may not have the cache of a magic bullet. But it would continue to promote the importance of genomic work and enhance the possibility that it may lead to translational successes. And while it is assumed that the process will be laborious and uncertain, it would also offer a much stronger promise that we will have in place the delivery of interventions that can change the lives of children today while we search for more potent cures for tomorrow.

Author Index

Subject Index

E

Q

R